Time's Stop in Savannah

Also by Ted R. Spivey

A Manual of Style (with Kenneth M. England)
Religious Themes in Two Modern Novelists
The Humanities in the Contemporary South
The Renewed Quest
The Coming of the New Man
The Journey Beyond Tragedy
Revival: Southern Writers in the Modern City
*The Writer as Shaman: The Pilgrimages of Conrad Aiken and
    Walker Percy* (Mercer University Press)
To Die in Atlanta: Poems of the Civil War and After
Beyond Modernism: Toward a New Myth Criticism
Conrad Aiken: A Priest of Consciousness (with Arthur Waterman)
A City Observed: Poems of the New Age
Flannery O'Connor: The Woman, The Thinker, The Visionary
  (Mercer Univeristy Press)
Airport: America Rediscovered

Time's Stop in Savannah

Conrad Aiken's Inner Journey

Ted R. Spivey

MERCER UNIVERSITY PRESS
Macon, Georgia

ISBN 0-86554-533-2
MUP/H408

PS3501
I5
Z87
1997

Time's Stop in Savannah
Conrad Aiken's Inner Journey
by
Ted R. Spivey

Mercer University Press
6316 Peake Road
Macon, Georgia 31210-3960

The paper used in this publication meets the minimum
requirements of American National Standard for Information
Sciences — Permanence of Paper for Printed Library Materials,
ANSI Z39.48–1984.

Library of Congress Cataloging-in-Publication Data

Spivey, Ted Ray, 1927 —
  Time's Stop in Savannah : Conrad Aiken's inner journey / Ted R. Spivey.
  pp.
  Includes bibliographical references.
  ISBN 0-86554-533-2 (alk. paper)
  1. Aiken, Conrad, 1889-1973--Psychology. 2. Authors, American-Georgia--Savannah--
Psychology. 3. Authors, American--20th century-Psychology. 4. Modernism (literature)--
United States.
5. Authorship--Psychological aspects. 6. Parent and child in literature. 7. Psychoanalysis
and literature. 8. Savannah (Ga.)--Biography. 9. Psychology in literature. 10. Death in
literature. 11. Creative ability.
  I. Title.
PS3501.I5Z87 1997
818'.5209--dc21

Contents

Introduction 1

1. Time's Stop in Savannah: Conrad Aiken and Psychoanalysis 7

2. Aiken in Savannah and Cambridge 21

3. Literary Comrades and Perilous Lovers 39

4. Aiken and Eliot: Poetry's Nature and Function 57

5. The Poet as Pilgrim 75

6. Fictional Descent into Hell 91

7. Apocalypse: *Ushant* and the Preludes 107

8. Visions of a Modern Romantic: Santayana, Nietzsche, and the Philosophic Mind 127

9. Immanence and Transcendence 141

Epilogue: The Quest for Home 161

for

Lewis P. Simpson

Introduction

The chief purpose of this study of Conrad Aiken and his work is to explore the author's literary, spiritual, and psychological development in order to throw new light on the pilgrimage of a significant modern man of letters. In the process of examining this neglected and often rediscovered writer I hope also to throw some new light on Savannah, the city of his birth, and on the continuing quest of writers to reveal the inner depths of the individual in their work.

Shortly after the turn of the century a nightmarish event shattered young Conrad's relatively happy life in the center of Savannah. At the age of eleven, already showing signs of great intelligence and some literary ability, Conrad discovered the dead bodies of his parents one morning after hearing pistol shots. His father had murdered his mother and then taken his own life. Time for the young Aiken seemed to stop in the first horrible moments of this discovery. As I seek to show in the study that follows, Aiken's discovery of his dead parents in their beautiful house on Oglethorpe Avenue--in a city that itself was trying to make time stop--led him eventually to a deep study of the new Freudian psychology. In time, Freud's insights would become a key factor in Aiken's search for both literary fame and his even deeper inner journey in search of mental and psychic stability. I will also seek to show how this inner search for reintegration of soul and personality led him on a journey that involved the gradual discovery of a cosmic power at the center of the soul. His quest then became not only a search for psychic stability, but also for the power of human creativity. In his work these creative powers are often symbolized by what for the poet was a kind of cosmic music at the heart of nature and of human existence.

Aiken's first important poem, "Music I Heard with You," records his discovery in art and love of a cosmic music that can restore health. The poem became one of his few popular works, yet he turned away from it because its style was not, he believed, representative of what he could do at his best. Not until middle age would he understand his own insights into the deepest elements in his art--that awareness of the possibilities in every soul for a creative life. But to begin with, Aiken had to deal with his own psychic suffering.

Aiken's early years of creativity, which began shortly after his graduation from Harvard University, dealt largely with his legacy of psychic agony. Eventually, he explored this agony in poems, stories, novels, and in one of the great American literary autobiographies, *Ushant.* Along the way he would be deeply drawn to the works of Freud as a way of explaining the profound problems in his own life and family. Freud, he said, many times, was "in everything I wrote." Yet Jung and other members of Freud's inner circle, Alfred Adler and Otto Rank in particular, were also important in Aiken's life and work. Depth psychology, as I seek to show, was always present in Aiken's inner journey, or "pilgrimage" as he called it, and helped to guide him to the ceative powers in his psyche.

I interviewed Aiken a number of times from 1965 through 1969, and often asked him about his literary connections with depth psychology. He would talk freely about his debt to Freud but little about the others of Freud's circle whose work had had some influence on him. In 1965, sitting in his Savannah house on Oglethorpe Avenue, next door to the house where he grew up, when I first asked him about the use of Jung in his work, he said simply, "Jung is too mythopoeic." Aiken had little desire to discuss Carl Jung's work because I believe his admiration for Freud was so great that he did not want to say much about the disciple who eventually became his master's chief rival. But as I have pointed out in several essays on Aiken, Jung's work is needed to explain a number of symbols in Aiken's later work, particularly in *Ushant*. In fact, as I will later suggest, Jung's use of the symbol of the *mandala* is directly related in some of Aiken's work to the use of cosmic music as a means of pointing to the reintegration of the psyche.

Jung himself after his break with Freud always proclaimed the supreme importance of his master's work, but he was careful to say that Freud's psychology dealt chiefly with problems of sexuality. His own psychology, he said, was best suited for the problems of people beyond thirty-five when sexuality becomes less important than the problem of integrating the total personality so that fruitful life can be found in those years when the sexual powers begin to wane. Americans in particular have taken to Freud more than to the other great figures of psychoanalysis because for them increasingly in the twentieth century sexuality seems to be the greatest of human problems. Yet as the nation itself has grown more mature, problems of the second half of life have also been examined on deeper levels.

Aiken himself was forced to take Freud very seriously because for him sexual problems were particularly important. He was clearly the victim of an oedipus complex, and the struggles leading to the early death of his parents may also have been related to this problem. But Aiken also believed he should take on the problems of the second half of life, and this he did in his search for visions of harmony, particularly as he found these visions in music and poetry.

For an understanding of Aiken's relationship to music I am indebted to Professor Charmenz S. Lenhart, a leading authority in this century on the subject of music and American poetry. Professor Lenhart also knew Aiken in the years after World War II when he was poet-in-residence at the Library of Congress. I am indebted to her both for her understanding of Aiken's awareness of music as well as for information she gave me concerning the poet's use of Jung to interpret his own dreams. She observed that in conversations with him about dreams that he often seemed to place more weight on a Jungian interpretation of his own dreams than on a Freudian interpretation. Applying Professor Lenhart's views to a study of much of Aiken's later poetry, I have come to the conclusion that Aiken's awareness of his own vision of wholeness, which appears in some of his best poetry and in his autobiography, was linked to the mythic aspects of Jung's psychology, which he seemed reluctant to discuss with me on more than one occasion. I believe that his reluctance was due to his steadfast loyalty to Freud as the great psychoanalyst of the century. Nevertheless, as Aiken began to achieve at least a limited wholeness in his later life and work, he was increasingly drawn to use of images of wholeness in his work because these images expressed his own psychic development after forty.

This psychic development is in a sense paralleled by a postwar renaissance in Aiken's early hometown of Savannah. A popular book about Savannah that has brought thousands of tourists to the city since its publication in 1994, John Berendt's *Midnight in the Garden of Good and Evil*, records many of the facts of the Savannah renaissance that began in the fifties and that by the nineties had made the city one of the great tourist centers of the nation. As Berendt points out, Aiken as a part-time resident of the city made a genuine contribution to this renaissance. I observed in my conversations with Aiken during the late sixties that his involvement with the city of his birth was still profound and that he found the atmosphere there intellectually and spiritually invigorating; in short, he was experiencing a sense of psychic rebirth in a city that was no longer a place of painful memories. It had become for him a city that he and his wife Mary deeply loved, one they often took walks in and drives when he was no longer so active.

Aiken told my wife and me how he and Mary liked to take a daily ride to see the ships on the Savannah River. Once, he said, they saw a ship whose name was "Cosmos Mariner." When they returned to the home on Oglethorpe Avenue, they looked up the destination of the ship and found the word "Unknown." Aiken said he then told his wife he wanted "Cosmos Mariner-Destination Unknown" to be his epitaph. It is now, along with the words "Give my love to the world." I will return to this most interesting epitaph later, but would now suggest that Aiken indeed saw himself as a man of the cosmos moving after death toward an unkown destination. The epitaph sums up his sense of his own cosmic vision, which springs directly from the Unitarianism of his maternal grandfather, Alfred Claghorn Potter, famous New England preacher and friend of Emerson. Even before he returned to Savannah, Aiken had found again the unifying vision of Potter, and moved into a cosmic view of human existence. But I believe he was led to this view gradually by Potter and many others, C. G. Jung and his friend of fifty years, T. S. Eliot, among others. But I am now at the center of the theme I will pursue in the book that follows. In connection with Savannah I would like to suggest two other facts concerning Aiken and the city. His last book, *Thee,* was written in Savannah, and is a book about his encounter with God.

Finally, one of Berendt's chief points about Savannah is that attending and giving parties is the central fact of this city's life. Aiken's brilliant and sought-after parents went to many parties in the city, and one of the things most deeply disturbing to Aiken's father shortly before time stopped for him and his wife was the fact that his wife, he thought, was going to too many parties. The murder-suicide of these two grew from far more than a rage for parties, but that too was part of the equation.

Brendt's book on Savannah, which in just two years time had sold a million copies, is but one of many indications that contemporary readers are extremely interested in the cultural manifestations--or lack of them--in the modern and newly-emerging postmodern cities of the world. Both in this and another work on Savannah-native Flannery O'Connor, I have sought to explain some of the many connections between visionary creative writers in our time and the complicated urban environments in which they often worked. Now, in a time when the creativity of Western culture itself has been called into question, it is necessary to study the ways great artists draw support from their urban environments and how they manage to contribute to the cultures that in part support their efforts.

I write about literary artists as people in cultural relationships. Yet I do so in a period in which many academic critics deny the very existence of writers and other artists. For the followers of the "New Historicism" there are no writers, but only texts, which in turn produce more texts, presumably without human involvement. The so-called "high tech" literary criticism invokes a world where only technology exists. The people necessary to explain this are critics who assure this new "postmodern" world that traditional writers who took seriously their own hearts, minds, and souls as they worked to make sense of a difficult period in history really never existed. To these critics such writers seem to be some sort of illusion. Nevertheless, I think the human struggle to find both meaning and happiness in a culturally fragmented world will always be an important subject for many artists, and particularly so in times of sweeping change such as these, when one millennium is giving way to another.

In attacking "high tech" literary criticism, I do not mean to denigrate the criticism of deconstruction, which I make use of myself. Though often difficult to follow, especially as it has been enunciated by its leading exponent Jacques Derrida, deconstruction offers insight into a number of literary problems. But contemporary academic deconstruction argues that most modern literature is, and is nothing more than, a statement about the destruction of the modern age. Poets like Aiken, Eliot, and Yeats, however, give us visions of both destruction and the renewal of a creativity that may in time lead to new ways of life. In the work that follows I have sought always to keep before the reader an awareness of Aiken's visions of both destruction and creative renewal in both individuals and in society.

Deconstruction, so mysteriously and arcanely practiced in the European and American academies, seems to be another way of stifling individual thought. Derrida and others like him have shown, however, that a deconstructive attitude can valuably help rid us of dying thought systems that can make way for Joyce's affirmative "yes." This in turn opens up new ways of both living and thinking. Aiken, of course, never used the term "deconstruction" nor did he ever think of himself as an "existential" writer. But at his best he was certainly involved in literary pursuits that deconstructed dead systems in order to make way for renewed visions of creative human existence.

In the chapters that follow I have sought first to relate Aiken the poet and the human being to the modern psychoanalytic tradition. Then in the two chapters that follow I discuss his relations with some of the significant people and places of his life, first in Savannah and then in the larger world of New England, New York, and Great Britain. I discuss his close literary and personal relationship with T. S. Eliot, his friend of many years. Then in the next three chapters I explore the three great themes of his work: the poet as pilgrim, the descent into Hell, which dominates much of his fiction, and visions of apocalypse, which are developed in his mature works such as *The Preludes* and his autobiography, *Ushant*. Finally, in the last two chapters I deal with his most basic themes as they are connected with his philosophical, psychological, and religious viewpoints.

Many people have helped me in the writing of this book and in its final preparation for print. For their continuing encouragement I want to thank Mercer University Press Publisher Cecil P. Staton and my editors Jon Peede and Marc Jolley. I also want to thank for his encouragement a former editor of Mercer University Press, Marvin Bergman, who helped me understand some of the shamanic aspects of the similarities between Walker Percy and Conrad Aiken in a book of mine published earlier by Mercer, *The Writer as Shaman: The Pilgrimages of Conrad Aiken and Walker Percy*. For their help with certain Jungian concepts I am indebted to Richard Sugg and Joseph K. Davis. I am particularly indebted to Professors Davis, Arthur Waterman, and Douglas Robillard for supplying me with much information and help in our original project on Aiken that began in 1968 and was finally completed with the publication in 1990 of *Conrad Aiken: A Priest of Consciousness,* edited by Professor Waterman and myself. I am also indebted to many other Aiken scholars and general readers who still find Aiken to be delightful reading and with whom I have corresponded and whom I have met at conferences. For profound help with concepts relating myth to the psychology of Freud and Jung I am indebted to the writings and speeches of the late mythologist Joseph Campbell as well as to a number of lengthy conversations with this scholar who first made it possible for many of us to see how depth psychology could be used to write about myth and literature.

The dedication of this book is an acknowledgment of my many debts to Lewis P. Simpson, Boyd Professor and William A. Read Professor, emeritus, of English Literature at Louisiana State University. As editor of *The Southern Review* he published my first article on Aiken in 1972 and has since then provided me with much encouragement in scholarly endeavors. My debt to my wife Julie is far too great to mention. She was with me on all of my trips to interview Aiken; she has continued to be a source of understanding and knowledge concerning Aiken's many depths, both psychological and otherwise, and has continued to guide my reading in many areas that have helped me to bring understanding to the life and work of this great poet of Georgia and of America.

Chapter 1

Time's Stop in Savannah:
Conrad Aiken and Psychoanalysis

Conrad Aiken was one of the most complex men of letters America has ever known, so complex that he is still not very well understood even after the first volume of his letters appeared in 1978. These letters, edited by Joseph Killorin, stimulated a new interest in Aiken's letters as Killorin, Aiken's long-time associate and a retired professor of English at Armstrong University in Savannah, began to write the official biography. What the letters indicated was a complexity of personality and of literary associations that reminded many readers more of a European man of letters than of an American poet. The letters also reminded many that Aiken is still one of the most neglected figures in modern American literature.

With renewed interest in the works of Sigmund Freud in this last decade of the twentieth century, it is time to once again evaluate the work of a writer who as short story writer, novelist, and poet put Freud and depth psychologists of the psychoanalytical movement that Freud launched at the turn of this century at the very center of his work. Frederick J. Hoffman, a significant critic in the area of literature and psychoanalysis, published in 1962 a major book examining Aiken's use of psychoanalysis as a means of exploring his own mind and soul. Aiken, Hoffman asserts, reveals in his writing a deep concern for the "problem and paradoxes" of the "isolated ego."[1] Aiken worked out a strategy, Hoffman tells us, for dealing with these problems in his own life. That strategy, Hoffman suggests, is the psychoanalytic method, and it is best exemplified in Aiken's novel *Great Circle.* It is, he continues, to be found in most of his best poetry and fiction.

Also in 1962 there appeared another book-length work on Aiken, Jay Martin's *Conrad Aiken: A Life of His Art.*[2] This book, written by a man who

---

[1] Frederick J. Hoffman, *Conrad Aiken* (New York: Twayne, 1962) 146.

[2] Jay Martin, *Conrad Aiken: A Life of His Art* (Princeton: Princeton University Press, 1962). The theme of Martin's book is that Aiken has a deep connection with leading Romantics like Goethe and Emerson, but the author tends to neglect the modernist side of Aiken's work as well as Aiken's own inner journey to discover the powers of human creativity. Martin wrote his book with Aiken's help, but the poet was disappointed in the

knew Aiken, emphasizes a major aspect of the author's work that is largely ignored by Hoffman. That aspect is Aiken's reliance on nineteenth-century literature, particularly the work of Emerson. Martin emphasizes the value of seeing Aiken as a representative man in the Emersonian sense of that term, one who carries on in his life and work certain basic values of Western culture. Martin has some good points to make. After all, Aiken's maternal grandfather was a Unitarian minister who was Emerson's friend. Aiken carried his grandfather Potter's sermons with him everywhere he went and read them most of his life. The Unitarian vision clearly is to be found in much of Aiken's best work. This vision, as I will suggest, is in some ways related to certain psychological insights found in the work of another psychoanalyist, C. G. Jung. Aiken makes it clear many times that Freud was his chief psychoanalytical influence but that he was also influenced by several of Freud's closest associates, C. G. Jung and Alfred Adler chief among them.

But before outlining some of the ways in which Freud did influence Aiken very profoundly, it is necessary to call attention to the fact that Aiken, like many writers, was influenced by other writers who also used the insights of psychoanalysis in their work. Chief among these for Aiken was James Joyce, whose stream-of-consciousness techniques were early adopted by Aiken. In fact Aiken's novel that made good use of the stream-of consciousness technique, *Blue Voyage*, appeared only one year after the publication of *Ulysses*. In much of his best work, particularly in several of his short stories, Aiken also used the technique of the small, imaginative insight that Joyce would call the epiphany. As in Joyce's fiction, Aiken's epiphanies would provide brief glimpses into the kind of transcendental reality of which Freud knew little but that Jung made much of. In fact, Joyce was particularly pleased when Jung early recognized the greatness of *Ulysses*, and Joyce eventually came to know Jung personally.

Aiken, who lived many of the years between the two world wars in England, would in fact seek to mediate between the new writers of Britain, particularly T. S. Eliot, who was a friend of his since his Harvard days, and the young writers of America, many of whom were more deeply drawn to Freud than to any of the other depth psychologists. In fact, it is Freud that Aiken was first most drawn to, and there was very good reason for this. Aiken had from an early age certain profound problems of the psyche that

---

result because the book does not deal with Aiken's inner journey.

Freud had begun to deal with from the beginning of his early break with other psychic healers of his time. As two of Aiken's greatest stories, *Silent Snow, Secret Snow* and *Strange Moonlight*, reveal in telling detail, the author had problems with an oedipus complex and with a deep antagonism to his father. These two stories both point toward the most traumatic event of Aiken's life, the murder-suicide of his parents.

Most accounts of the poet's life and work begin with a statement concerning Aiken's father, half mad, who shot his wife in the midst of a loud argument and then turned his pistol on himself, the two bodies being discovered by eleven-year-old Conrad Aiken. From Aiken's own works and from autobiographical references in stories and poems, we know that the boy had been experiencing the increasing violence of his parents for many months. In 1901, when divorce was uncommon, few people knew clearly what is today common knowledge dispensed by pyschological counselors: children are called upon to mediate the disputes of warring parents. When mediation fails and separation occurs, the young mediator bears a burden of guilt for what he believes to be his own failure. Not only was Aiken mediating between his parents--his mother shortly before her death begging him to protect her--as the oldest of four children he had to mediate between two warring parents and his frightened siblings. The strain of it all could well have broken the young Aiken, and, in one sense, he spent the rest of his life recovering from his early suffering.

In 1932 Aiken would himself attempt suicide, saved only by the quick efforts of his second wife, Clarissa S. Lorenz. That same year a close friend, the poet John Gould Fletcher, had attempted suicide and was subsequently committed to an asylum. Aiken, however, managed to continue his own efforts at self-analysis as he discovered that it was necessary to recall from his unconscious mind the repressed chaotic emotions of early childhood. Thus it is little wonder that he was early a follower of Freud, who with his new method of psychic healing that he called psychoanalysis, had shown the world ways to bring back to the conscious mind repressed unconscious contents that were threatening to destroy the individual. Freud also believed that through dream analysis and through methods of talking about one's psychic problems it was possible to restore the mind to health.

What Freud offered moderns was a way of ridding themselves of dangerous psychic contents. Even the chaotic elements in the unconscious, Aiken learned from Freud, could be used to challenge the pilgrim like himself who sought to live in the glow of the power of Eros, which made possible fruitful love relations as well as a balanced life that acknowledged the demands of both the conscious and the unconscious sides of humans. Freud, who believed that writers had much to teach psychoanalysts, kept a copy of Aiken's novel *Great Circle* on his waiting room table. In Aiken he saw a writer who could teach both him and his patients something about the unconscious mind. He wanted to analyze Aiken, but when the author was on board ship to go to Vienna to receive an analysis, to be paid for by the poet Hilda Doolittle, he met one of Freud's followers, Eric Fromm. Fromm told him that no one who did not really need psychoanalysis should offer himself up to the couch. Thus what might have been a rich event in the history of literature and psychoanalysis failed to occur.

What Aiken discovered in his own self-analysis was that all of his life he had been mediating between life and death, between the desire to embrace life and the desire to take his own life. He found also that he had been trying most of his life to return to the comfort of the remembered mother and that to achieve his own creativity meant overcoming the mother image with new powerful images of creation. Freud himself, having early posited the pleasure principle of love and sexuality as the foundation of his work, later posited the death principle as another central idea in his thinking. But Freud, like Aiken, was, in spite of being a modern scientist, also a Romantic. In his last important work, *Civilization and its Discontents*, Freud sees modern life as being simply too complex and repressive to sustain human creativity. The answer he points to, a much simpler way of life, springs primarily from the philosophy of Rousseau. In this philosophy he is not so different from Tolstoy, who came to believe in a new and simple society based on many of Rousseau's principles.

The limitations of psychoanalysis, which Freud began to realize late in life, are made clear in Erich Fromm's book *Sigmund Freud's Mission*. "Psychoanalysis," Fromm writes, "became a surrogate religion for the urban middle and upper-middle classes." While giving Freud great credit for his work in creating the movement, he makes this point against it: "psychoanalysis became a substitute satisfaction for a deep human yearning, that of finding a meaning to life, of being in genuine touch with reality, of doing away with the distortions and projections that put a veil between reality and ourselves."[3] Fromm and other figures in the movement--C. G. Jung, Alfred Adler, Otto Rank as well as later figures long after the Freud's

---

[3]Erich Fromm, *Sigmund Freud's Mission* (New York: Grove Press, 1967) 117.

death--have all sought to go beyond analysis alone to the discovery of a reality principle that would fulfill the deepest psyhic and social needs of humans. Aiken himself would be part of this movement that I believe essentially to be a form of modern Romanticism, a movement that seeks to discover the creative principle at the center of life, in both the conscious and unconscious minds. Adler sought creativity essestially in the work of individuals with others in society, and Rank believed that creativity could be found in the search for heroism and even immortality, which he believed was inherent in existence. Jung believed in the search for a creativity inherent in what he called the "archetypes," particularly that of the Self, the creative principle at the center of humanity.

Aiken, as I will continue to suggest in later chapters, sought creativity in a number of ways. He was very much wedded to modern science. His father had been a doctor and a scientific inventor, and he never escaped that influence, which made him admire Freud both as a scientist and one of the great men of his time. But he was also a follower of his grandfather Potter's Unitarianism, which taught him to seek joy and creativity, and with them to overcome the death wish that is part of all human existence.

I would suggest that it is time to take into account the attempts of many writers in the modernist tradition to balance the destructiveness in their own lives and the times they live in with the streams of creativity they could discover both in themselves and in their societies. Aiken is by no means the greatest of these writers who managed to achieve enough balance to continue being creative at least into middle age, but he is the writer who more than any other in this category revealed his many attempts to stay afloat in his creative work. The reason is, I think, he had more problems to overcome than did most writers.

Aiken never overcame all his psychic problems, but then who does? But he was able to continue his work into old age and to make a deep impression as a man of letters and as a person involved in human existence on many people who knew him. And yet his second wife, Clarissa, in her book *Lorelei Two: My Life with Conrad Aiken* calls Aiken a "narcissist" and goes on to claim that she found in discussing her life with "other artists' wives" that "the American male author" is "a chauvinist magnified a thousandfold." "His pleasures," she continues, "were taken mostly with male friends, his mate regarded as a sex object more often than not, and excluded from his intellectual life." She concludes her tirade with an attack on all artists: "What ordinary mortals can't swallow about artists is the ravaging of others, but the daemon will continue to destroy with impunity."[4] One may well sympathize with the difficulties of Lorenz's often painful life with of Aiken. She was the wife of the middle period of Aiken's life, and at the peak of this period, in the thirties, he often came close to destroying himself. On one occasion of attempted suicide he probably owes his life to his second wife's timely intervention. In one judgment of Aiken, Clarissa is most surely wrong. This is when she says simply, "Nothing could have shocked him out of that childhood numbness." At the end of her book she in effect negates this judgment by writing about meeting him long after their divorce. She left him, she says of this event in 1960, with the following thoughts: "The amenities over, we smiled, shook hands, and went our separate ways, he with that purposeful air of authority I once thought so captivating, I with mixed feelings, missing a chance to say the obvious--that living with a poet who touched so many lives had enriched my own life immeasurably."[5]

Aiken's childhood numbness, part of which he had with him all his life, did not prevent him from enriching the lives of others. The numbness began when his parents began their endless quarrels and reached a climax when time itself seemed to stop that morning he found their bodies. Yet that numbness did not prevent him from going immediately to a police station to get help for himself and his younger brothers and sister, all of whom had so suddenly been orphaned. All of his life he would feel this numbness come upon him, would experience that moment of time seeming to stop. Yet he found ways to go on past much of this numbness; even Clarissa notes the value of Aiken's journey of continuing creativity.

More than from anyone else who knew Aiken that I interviewed, I learned the most about Aiken's continuing growth into openness and love from his third wife, the most fortunate of the three wives because she married Aiken when he was beginning to make peace with his inner demons. Mary Hoover, a painter and significant artist in her own right, told me in 1979, six years after Aiken's death the origin of the second epitaph on his tombstone. Some months before he died, Aiken was in bed sick and Mary asked before going out if she could get him anything. He declined but said "Give my love to the world." Later after he recovered, she told him what he had said and then she told him she would put these words on his tombstone.

---

[4]Clarissa M. Lorenz, *Lorelei Two: My Life with Conrad Aiken* (Athens: University of Georgia Press, 1983) 219.

[5] Ibid., 220.

Unless one fully realizes what Bonaventure Cemetery meant to Aiken and what his own final statement to the world in this cemetery meant, he cannot understand the depth of the poet's feeling about both those closest to him and about the city that was the central place of his life.

Of the depths of Aiken's personal affections there can be no doubt. We see these depths in his early poetry, but the moments of them are presented as being brief. But in his later life, especially with his third wife Mary, they become stronger. There are a number of reasons for this, and in several conversations I had with Aiken in the sixties, he admitted to rediscovering earlier relationships that had been partially or totally broken. Chief among these was his friendship with T. S. Eliot, which I will refer to again in later chapters. Aiken explained to me in some detail how the two friends had at first drifted apart in the early twenties when Eliot began to achieve wide fame with the publication of *The Waste Land*. At times in his discussions of the early Eliot, pain would actually come into Aiken's voice. The greatest pain he revealed in his discussion of Eliot in the twenties appeared when he talked about his friend's becoming an Anglican. Aiken is quite clear about these and similar matters in *Ushant*. But in other conversations with Aiken I would hear tones of deep feeling when he described their reunification after Eliot remarried. Aiken seemed to attribute much of the change in Eliot to the profound effect Eliot's second wife Vivien had upon him. After Eliot's death Vivien visited Aiken in Savannah, and he went to great lengths to tell me how deeply touched he was by her friendship.

Peter Ackroyd in his biography of Eliot discusses at length the changes that occurred in Eliot's nature after his second marriage. On a visit to America in 1958 with his wife Vivien, Eliot evinced a happiness that was expressed quite openly. And Ackroyd continues, "In Cambridge he publicly embraced his old friend, Conrad Aiken, moving Aiken almost to tears."[6] When talking to me of this new Eliot, Aiken would in fact approach tears. But clearly the changes in Eliot were due to more than a new wife. Eliot, as Ackroyd suggests, had found a new life. Eliot himself in two public readings had said that he had lost touch with the "young man who had written the earlier poetry." Ackroyd then adds this: "It would be more accurate to say that he had escaped from him. Just as he had the ability to compartmentalize his life, so he also seemed able to slough off the weight of

---

[6]Peter Ackroyd, *T. S. Eliot: A Life* (New York: Simon and Schuster, 1984) 323-324.

the past and begin anew."[7]

One wonders how Eliot found strength to begin a new life so late in his career. I think in fact both Aiken and Eliot had discovered the necessity of finding new depths of a hidden love in their cramped psyches. Eliot himself admits as much in his last play, *The Elder Statesman*, a work that is about, in part, the rediscovery of a lost friend who resembles Aiken in many ways, though there is an attempt to disguise the character. The character who is clearly Eliot in the play, Lord Claverton, at last finds that he can begin to love and with love can begin to be happy. The reason, he tells us, that he can begin to love is that he has sloughed off "The man that I pretended to myself that I was."[8]

Eliot stayed as far away as he could from psychology in all of its varied schools of thought. Aiken, of course, was the opposite. He above most other American poets needed the help of Freud and his disciples. For Aiken what was deepest in Freud was his search for love in all its forms, sexual included, and in his awareness of the problems caused by the possessive love of parents who could not let go their own warped visions of themselves, which in large part had been imposed upon then by their parents. As I will suggest in later chapters, Aiken used Freud freely in most of his work but he also drew from other depth psychologists and from philosophy and religion because he believed that psychology in all its forms was one of the great expressions of Western civilization. Thus he did not take it to be some kind of method that in itself could save all humanity, nor did he believe Freud did.

As he grew older Aiken inevitably became interested in the psychology of Freud, Adler, Jung, and Rank because they delved into the problem Eliot wrote about in his last play, *The Elder Statesman*, the problem of how to slough off that person or persons that you pretended to yourself you were. And after the sloughing off process occurs there is the need to discover and to use the powers of love and creativity that exist in even the most wounded of souls. Aiken was able to recover enough creativity to bring forth mature works like *Ushant* and *The Coming Forth by Day of Osiris Jones*. When James Joyce saw this latter title he realized it contained the germ of his still unpublished last work, *Finnegans Wake*. That germ, or better, essential idea, is that humanity in a renewed inner journey in our time is even now beginning to slough off an old self and to find a new and creative self.

---

[7] Ibid.

[8] T. S. Eliot, *The Elder Statesman* (New York: Farrar, Straus and Company, 1964) 128.

Aiken's pioneering attempts to use various schools of modern psychology and psycho- analysis to search for his own creativity did not desert his first psychological master, Freud. In fact, he continued to work with the great problems that Freud posed for modern man, which was how to get past the stifling powers of possessive parents, to get past those two conditions he called the oedipus complex and the electra complex. Aiken to the end of his life struggled with an oedipus complex, but the fact that he did not let it overcome him can be seen in his creative life, which could be observed in the richness of his conversation up to the end of his life. I myself found his conversation to be the richest literary talk I ever experienced and so did many others. To be caught in in the entanglement of an oedipus or electra complex is to be either unable to talk in a meaningful manner or to be possessive and self-centered in conversation. And yet critics are once again, as we are entering a new and threatening century, beginning to point to Aiken and similar writers as being figures doomed to psychological torment.

In 1988 the first volume of Edward Butscher's two volume biography of Aiken appeared, entitled *Conrad Aiken: Poet of White Horse Vail*, and in it the author does an excellent job of examining the profound influence of psychoanalysis on Aiken. He also deals with the ways in which Aiken used his dreams in writing some of his best work, referring, for instance, to "Conrad's recall of dreams in precise detail, as a storehouse for many future poems and tales."[9] Butscher's biography of Sylvia Plath is a masterpiece of psychological analysis because the author's Freudian method fits her life and work very well. But the Freudian method alone will not explain much of Aiken's life and work because he was influenced by the other depth psychologists I have already discussed and because his life did not end in suicide as did Plath's. Butscher's Freudian method fails him completely when he writes that "The tragic central reality of Conrad's inner growth, which made him the lyric poet he became, was that the next stage in his psychological development, the essential move from metaphoric expressions of self-pity into genuine love, never materialized."[10] I have already suggested that Aiken indeed had moved into a stage of genuine love. Otherwise, he could not have written *Ushant* and other books. He would in fact have

---

[9] Edward Butscher, *Conrad Aiken: Poet of the White Horse Vale*, Vol. 1 (Athens: University of Georgia Press, 1988) 198.

[10] Ibid, 7.

appeared as a kind of monster to those who knew him, which he did not.

When Butscher thus writes that "Aiken would remain frozen in a narcissistic phase that did not permit him to enter other consciousnesses, that kept him forever inside the child's shell of self,"he is actually expressing a view of writers and literature that is prominent in the last two decades of this century.[11] It is a view based on that vague and often used term "deconstruction." This term has many meanings, but I take it generally to refer to a growing sense of destructiveness that is in the air. It represents an inevitable feeling that appears at the end of every century and is probably greater than it has been for many centuries because we are also at the end of a millennium. In fact, in my own work on Aiken I have used the word at times because the poet was deeply aware of the fact of deconstruction as a spirit in his own life and in the life of that seemingly placid decade before World War I, a time that was secretly preparing itself for modern warfare, the most destructive behavior ever conceived. Inevitably the greatest spirits in the arts-- and Aiken was one of these--must deal with the "deconstruction" of what for them is both the joy and the horror of their own age, that is, the culture within which they swim and have their beings as creators.

In the 1990s we are more aware than ever of the growing power of deconstructive elements, hopefully making way for new creativity. We now have a new biography of Malcolm Lowry, that genius who wrote the greatest modern novel on the alcholic personality, *Under The Volcano*. Aiken's role in Lowry's life is made to seem sinister, which it was not, but then the author himself must cling to his deconstructive sense in writing it. In 1995 appeared a significant book that looks at deconstructing personalities in modern poetry with new vision. This is Helen Vendler's *The Given and the Made: Strategies of Poetic Redefinition*. The central poets of this study are Robert Lowell and John Berryman, two of the leading "confessional" poets in a school that made a strong mark on the sixties and seventies. Aiken himself in this period was regarded as a forerunner of this school, and, in fact, Aiken was a major influence on Berryman. When in 1954 Berryman, jobless and almost penniless in Minneapolis, began his major work, *The Dream Songs*, he discovered Aiken's *Ushant*, a work that revealed how a poet guided by his dreams could extend his career beyond disorder and early sorrow to find new powers of creativity that would carry him past his neurotic problems, which

---

[11] Ibid., 27.

included among other things a strong impulse toward suicide. Berryman was unable, in spite of the brilliance of *The Dream Songs*, to find the path beyond suicide, as Aiken did, and eventually he jumped to his death off a Minneapolis bridge in 1972.

The search for that path is still essentially a kind of Romantic quest. In fact, as we proceed to the end of the last decade of this century, it is possible to perceive how deeply certain Romantic currents are embedded in the best work of many literary figures. Romanticism, which at its best deals with an inner search for identity and for hidden emotional and psychic powers, is still a way of life for some artists even at this century's end. Both depth psychologists like Freud and Jung and new poets like Eliot and Aiken began their careers with visions that were essentially modernist, but as their careers continued over the years a search for the powers of regeneration bringing with them new emotional depths can often be found.

Thus in time Freud would write that it was not sex alone he was concerned with but the total love life of man. Rousseau, often called the father of Romanticism, would by the time Freud wrote *Civilization and its Discontents* be the central figure in the great psychologist's deepest meditations. After his early creative years of the hard modernist images of his first major phase, Eliot in his dramas and above all in *Four Quartets* would explore the never ending human journey in search of love. And Conrad Aiken, his friend and sometimes enemy of more than fifty years, would continue even from his earliest years to seek in and through his art to reveal the inner journey in search of that power of love that he believed was necessary for for the preservation of life itself. He more than most of the poets of his century needed this power to overcome that agony of time's stop --experienced in that house where he first knew a profound but fleeting parental love. And in his best work Aiken revealed by taking the Unitarian-Transcendentalist path of Emerson and Thoreau, he could achieve a measure of wisdom and psychic development of the kind we see in Goethe and a handful of other artists since 1750.

Helen Vendler has recently given us a study of what often happens to creative artists and many others as a way of life that is associated with a particular century begins to wane. Inevitably artists, philosophers, and mystics begin to sense this change, and, if they find the creative center within themselves, they give us works that point the way to a creative future and even provide some of the energies necessary to bring this future into being. But in many cases the new creators must heal themselves in order to present their own visions of a new and creative age. That Aiken was successful can be seen in the fact that he did heal himself on a long journey that he called a pilgrimage. He began this pilgrimage, as he freely admits in *Ushant* and in conversations with a number of people, including myself, with the help of Freud and psychoanalysis, but he also drew heavily from Jung, Adler, and Rank. Yet he never limited himself to modern psychoanalysis. He drew heavily also from Santayana and his grandfather Potter, the Unitarian minister that he once told me might have been more influential than anyone. Also he drew much from poets who themselves had continued their journey into old age, among them T. S. Eliot and William Carlos Williams.

I had the good fortune once to hear Aiken express himself in one sentence about his life's journey, which he believed was a journey toward an ever more inclusive personal consciousness. In fact, Aiken called himself a "priest of consciousness." I was talking to Aiken in 1965 about the difficulty of his life's journey. Suddenly I was moved to say, "There was so much suffering in it." He gave me one of his warm smiles and said: "And it all began right over there." He was pointing a finger at a wall of the room where he spoke. On the other side of that wall was the room, in the row house next door, where in 1901 his father had killed his mother and then himself, leaving an eleven-year-old boy to find the bodies.

Many others can also recall the warm Aiken of his ripe years after World War II. Charmenz S. Lenhart also recalls from her own conversations with Aiken a number of references to Jung, and I quote from one of her letters, concerning her observations of Aiken in the years after World War II: "I suspect I thought him more Jungian than Freudian because violence and death left such an imprint on him."[12] In a way this sentence sums up Aiken's use of psychoanalysis. Freud had been necessary, with his doctrine of the need to lift from the unconscious mind the contents of a wounded psyche so that they could be dealt with, but Jung had also been necessary to point to evidence in the dreams of everyone of a creative center--a Self, Jung called it, that could provide the creative energies to guide people past their early psychic wounds and could be a basis for a continuing development of mind and soul on the human inner journey.

Thus psychoanalysis as taught by various masters would help individuals get past those moments of time's stop, as in the case of Aiken's traumatic

---

[12] Letter from Charmenz S. Lenhart to Ted R. Spivey, December 10, 1995.

discovery of his dead parents. But it could also help to lift people above the strong powers of narcissism and the oedipus complex that make many at various moments want to cling to an admired image of oneself or of one's parents. But to seek to make time stop altogether, Aiken would continually discover, is to doom oneself to stasis and ultimately to chaos of soul and emotional sorrow. Like all of us Aiken was called upon to move past narcissism and his own oedipal feelings in order to find energies with which to love and to create. And a city, he found, also seeks to make time stop when it falls in love with itself. To go on living it must be reborn. It was Aiken's fortune, as his own rebirth slowly happened, to once again live in a beloved city, Savannah, that was reborn in the 1950s and that continued its growth through Aiken's old age, as it continues it even now.

Chapter 2

Aiken in Savannah and Cambridge

Conrad Aiken was intensely aware of what D. H. Lawrence called the spirit of place. In his two most anthologized works, "Tetélestai" and "Silent Snow, Secret Snow," an awareness of the spirit of Savannah and its environs is powerfully presented. Both works are concerned with Aiken's most deeply felt subject--extreme emotional pain--and yet the awareness of particular places in Savannah is nearly as strong as the author's presentation of psychic pain. In his best writing Aiken would seldom separate his remembrance of joy and sorrow from his feeling for places where he had experienced moments of intense emotion.

In his approach to his own and other people's emotions Aiken is clearly a Romantic, but in his handling of environments of emotion he is a realist. Aiken's literary roots are Romantic, but possibly he found it necessary to mediate between Romantic and realistic viewpoints in order not to be swept away by excesses of emotion. It was a strategy used by various modern Romantics--D. H. Lawrence, William Faulkner, Dylan Thomas, Malcolm Lowry--all writers Aiken admired. Unlike these four writers Aiken all his creative life used another method to temper his emotionalism; this method was the continuing cultivation of the philosophical mind expressed in the manner of symbolist poets. Sometimes the philosophical mind betrayed the artist in Aiken, causing some of his poetry to seem abstract and even sterile, but this long developed philosophical viewpoint was necessary to give meaning to a personal sorrow. The untimely collapse of many modern Romantics like Hart Crane or Dylan Thomas can be traced back to a failure to find any substantial philosophical or religious basis for their lives and work.

The two places most important in Aiken's personal growth are undoubtedly Cambridge, Massachussetts, and Savannah, Georgia. For the development of Aiken the poet, the professional writer, and the man of letters, Cambridge 'and Harvard University are the places where the teachers who set Aiken on the philosophical quest were discovered, George Santayana being the chief among them. Harvard was where his longest friendship with another poet, T. S. Eliot, first began. As a Harvard graduate, and the son of a Harvard graduate Aiken would see the university, above all of his other New England connections, as central to his life in the Northeast.

Yet Aiken first decided to become a poet in Savannah. In *Ushant* he recalls lying on the floor of the nursery reading the epigraph to the first chapter of *Tom Brown's School Days*: "I'm the poet of White Horse Vale, Sir, / With liberal notions under my cap." Conrad asked his father what the word "poet" meant only to find that his own parent had written poems. From that moment, Aiken says, he was determined to be a poet. Eventually he would move to England, live not far from White Horse Vale, and would in a big room of his house in Rye seek to create a room like the parlor of his Savannah house. He would also continue all his life to be a poet with liberal political ideas, even to the point of participating in Hubert Humphrey's presidential campaign of 1968 by writing a letter on behalf of his candidacy to the New York *Times*. He greatly prized a telephone call from Humphrey thanking him for his efforts. But from the South he absorbed more than childhood memories. He would, from early exposure to Southern culture, absorb a viewpoint that was in large part summed up in the career of Edgar Allan Poe.

Malcolm Cowley maintained that Emerson and Transcendentalism were at the heart of Aiken's life work, but Aiken acknowledged Poe as his chief literary forebear. Poe's stories were among his boyhood reading, and later Aiken would cite Poe as the first among American writers to be part of an international tradition--one, he believed, that he, Pound, and Eliot helped to maintain. Southern cities like Richmond, Charleston, and Savannah had always been drawn, far more than early Boston, to the literary culture of England and the Continent. Thus even as a child Aiken saw the poet as one who should be at home in both America and Europe. Yet, as Malcolm Cowley wrote in a seminal article in *The Southern Review*, "Conrad Aiken: From Savannah to Emerson," Aiken was "Boldest of all in his development of certain Transcendental notions."[1] The chief of these notions he inherited from his grandfather Potter: that man contains something divine in his make-up and that he can ultimately achieve unity with God. This is the core of what Aiken himself called the religion of consciousness, a term first used by F. O. Matthiessen in *Henry James: The Major Phase*, but one suggested to him by Aiken.

For Aiken true consciousness was, among other things, the awareness of the divine element in everyone. Yet this awareness, Aiken realized, is

---

[1]Malcolm Cowley, "Conrad Aiken: From Savannah to Emerson," *The Southern Review* 11 (Spring, 1975), 248.

fleeting for modern man. In Aiken's work we find few of those epiphanic moments one encounters in the best writing of Emerson, Thoreau, or Whitman, but the few we find are central to his work. Where mystical insight fails him, as it often does in his poetry, Aiken falls back on philosophical insight. An example of this is the beginning of *The Coming Forth By Day of Osiris Jones.* In this expressionistic drama, written in one of the most painful and creative years of his life, 1931, Aiken presents one of the many paradoxes that he continually wrote about: "Here we have sounded, angel!--/ O angel soul, O memory of man!--/ And felt the nothing that sustains our wings."[2] Aiken thus tells us that individuals have an angel soul but that we all, nevertheless, feel the nothingness that sustains these wings. Immediately the reader is plunged into the kind of paradox that Jean-Paul Sartre would explore early in World War II in his book *Being and Nothingness:* individuals are aware of a Being somewhere beyond everyday existence, yet they are plagued by a sense of nothingness, which for Sartre was largely a failure of expectations. But Sartre's own vision of nothingness comes in large part from his awareness of Poe and Baudelaire, that source of much of Aiken's vision, which includes much more than the New England voice Cowley hears.

Aiken continues in the work, after announcing the theme of nothingness, by presenting what he calls the "catalogue of things." But first he states the paradox of being and nothingness: "All in the maelstrom of the limbo caught, / and whirled concentric to the funnel's end, / sans number, and sans meaning, and sans purpose" (CP, 575). These lines are a statement of one side of the paradox, but this side is to be found in various forms in Aiken's work, so much so that some critics, like Frederick J. Hoffmann, have concluded that nothingness is at the center of the poet's vision. "The struggle with nothingness is unceasing," Hoffmann writes, further stating that the universe for Aiken is based on "Happenstance."[3] Hoffmann's concept of happenstance is similar to that popularized by Carl Sagan in his explanation of modern science called *Cosmos*: the universe is empty space filled with some material objects apprehended by the five human senses and chiefly

---

[2]Conrad Aiken, *Collected Poems* (New York: Oxford University Press, 1953), p.574. All references in the chapters that follow are to this edition and are hereinafter referred to as *CP*.

[3]Frederick J. Hoffman, *Conrad Aiken* (New York: Twayne Publishers, 1962), 137.

governed by chance, though humankind can influence small aspects of it by its own efforts. But Aiken's continuing Transcendentalism causes him in the first section of *The Coming Forth by Day of Osiris Jones* to state immediately the other side of the paradox: "save that the lack of purpose bears a name / the lack of meaning has a heart-beat and the lack of number wears a clock of stars" (CP, 575). Thus, for Aiken, the poet gives meaning and purpose to existence by the act of naming the stars and other parts of the universe, all of which are governed by a rhythm that calls to mind Albert Einsteins's statement concerning the necessity for physics to be based on what Leibnitz called "a pre-established harmony."[4] Aiken's grandfather and his Harvard mentor Santayana also held this view of physics and the other sciences; it remained always a basic concept in the poet's work. It is not so much that, as Hoffmann suggests, he always struggles with nothingness; rather, he takes into account the recurring human vision of nothingness and puts it along side the recurring vision of universal harmony. But because Aiken was chiefly a confessional poet, the essential question he raises in his work has to do with where harmony is to be found in the events of an individual's life, a question that includes a consciousness of both nothingness and harmony, a harmony that gives a sense of Being to existence. For this reason, I believe, the next section of his drama, called "The Things," deals with the two places that most affected his early life, Savannah and Cambridge Massachusetts.

That Aiken thought highly of "The Things" can be seen in the fact that he selected it for reading for a record in the Yale Series of Recorded Poets (DL 9128). The muted emotion in Aiken's voice while reading "The Things" is stronger than in most of his other recorded works. In fact, not to know Aiken's recordings is to miss a peculiar element of his emotional power that contains a blend of old-fashioned Romanticism and a modern awareness of an ever present human suffering and a sense of chaos. Above all else, "The Things" seeks to mediate between the early remembered scenes of childhood in Savannah--best symbolized by the opening line, "The house in Broad Street, red brick, with nine rooms"-- and the teenager's development in Cambridge, best summed up by a discovery of Shakespeare and by the

---

[4]Albert Einstein, *Essays in Science* (New York: The Wisdom Library, 1954), 4. In his essay called "Principles of Research" Einstein writes that "The longing to behold this pre-established harmony is the source of the inexhaustible patience and endurance with which Planck has devoted himself, as we see it, to the most general problems of our science ."

awareness of the opposite sex: "the new-found eyes no slumber could forget, / Vivien, the affliction of the senses" (*CP*, 576). Aiken thus announces the two great continuing facts of his entire life: the literary efforts, continued until death, which were greatly inspired by studying Shakespeare, and the struggle of the sexes, symbolized by a girl called Vivien and continued with three wives and various lovers. Yet at the end of "The Things," Aiken announces his most characteristic theme in his best known work, the remembrance of suffering. In the next-to-last stanza, Aiken speaks of the need to "remember now the red house with nine rooms / the graveyard with its trumpetvine and tombs." Once again he recalls Bonaventure Cemetery in Savannah, a place always important in his work and his thought, possibly as a symbol of death even more important than the living city of Savannah. Yet in keeping with his Egyptian theme in *The Coming Forth By Way of Osiris Jones*, the poet presents Bonaventure as a City of the Dead existing beside a city of the living. In the last stanza Aiken then records the emotional deprivation he suffered in New England: "[P]lay jackstones and let your jackstones be the stars that make Orion's galaxy so to deceive yourself until you move into that house whose tenants do not love." (*CP*, 577). Thus "The Things" ends with a memory of pain suffered in two American regions. This pain is the starting point of Aiken's continuing quest for personal and literary renewal, a renewal that could come for the individual only through encountering the immortal harmony, or divinity, existing at the core of each individual, as Aiken's inherited Transcendentalism taught. By the end of *Osiris Jones* Aiken has moved from his own individual suffering to the suffering of humanity and the transfiguration of humanity itself, symbolized by Osiris Jones, the god-man. Following the Egyptian Book of the Dead, Aiken shows the rejuvenation of man himself through his first accepting that chaos and sense of nothingness caused by the collapse of civilization and then through his discovery of that God whose coming forth into the light means the birth of a new man and a new age.

Aiken in 1931, at the time of writing *Osiris Jones,* faced once again his own remembered suffering, both in childhood and in his two marriages, as well as the suffering his native civilization was undergoing because of the Great Depression. The result, along with his attempted suicide (saved in the nick of time by his second wife Clarissa), was a poetic rebirth leading to one of his three greatest works, *Preludes to Memnon*, and to *Osiris Jones.* The year 1931 was similar to another seminal year, 1917, when with "Tetélestai" and other poems Aiken discovered his real voice. "Tetélestai," and "The Jig of Forslin"--his first Symphony, published in 1916--marked the beginning of a plunge into an unconscious mind loaded with repressed agonies. Only by facing his own suffering could Aiken then move on to a larger problem of how the modern artist can live and continue to be creative. The answer was partly that the artist should keep moving on a pilgrimage so that he would not imitate his earlier selves but would continually find sources of new creative power bubbling from within that would enable him to create works containing the freshness of psychic renewal.

Aiken's awareness of having begun a new creative life in 1917 was so strong that later he would leave his first volume, *Earth Triumphant and Other Tales in Verse* (1914), off his list of publications. The period beginning in 1931, which saw the publication of the first volume of Preludes, clearly marked for Aiken another new beginning, born out of present and past suffering. Curiously, his development had paralleled that of James Joyce. Both in their first periods wrote stories about early remembered events and then went on to write novels--*A Portrait of the Artist* and *Blue Voyage*--that revealed the artist's struggle to express himself in a society hostile to new and creative literary expression. Joyce would continue to write in *Ulysses* about the artist in the modern city as well as the underlying mythic correspondences with the ordinary events of modern life. In his fiction and poems of the twenties and thirties Aiken would also write about the struggles of the artist in the city, but with *Osiris Jones* he would break through to the essential insight of Joyce's *Finnegans Wake*. In his biography of Joyce, Richard Ellmann writes of Joyce's seeing the title and immediately thinking that this title, *The Coming Forth by Day of Osiris Jones,* in effect stated the theme of *Finnegans Wake*. Joyce was disturbed over possible similarities between the two works and felt impelled to read *Osiris Jones*, but was never able to do so. As it turned out, there was no problem because, unlike *Finnegans Wake, Osiris Jones* was only an opening statement of the greatest creative period of Aiken's life. Aiken, like Joyce, was driven to present the pilgrimage of man in search of the essential heroism at the heart of his being. But Aiken did not write a masterwork like the *Wake*. Instead, he wrote a series of works, beginning with the first volume of the Preludes and *Osiris Jones* and culminating in *Ushant* in 1952. Unlike Joyce, who died two years after the *Wake's* publication, Aiken would have another period of reduced creativity, a kind of coda in which he would solidify his understanding of New England and Savannah, thus writing several poems about his own rediscovery of various aspects of America and its major regions--the North, the South, and the West.

The comparison of Joyce and Aiken is always instructive because both men were in much of their work always trying to repossess themselves of the cities of their birth. Living as an exile in Paris, Joyce would spend his evenings tuned into the Dublin station on his radio, but he could not return. Aiken in 1936 would return to Savannah, having first begun to repossess himself of the city when as a student at Harvard he began to read his father's writing and could capture in it remembrances of his early Southern existence. When Aiken in 1936 walked out of the De Sota Hotel in downtown Savannah to begin the walk to the house on Oglethorpe Avenue, called Habersham Street when he lived there, he felt a current of emotion flowing within. In *Ushant* he would describe with a sense of awe this emotional overflow: "in the midst of this all-healing recapitulation, this triumph of repossession, flooding his veins with recollected beauty and power."[5] These words indicate that the return to Savannah marked a rebirth of the spirit for Aiken, a city that his biographer and close friend Joseph Killorin has called the lodestone of the poet's life. What Savannah meant personally to Aiken is best described in an article in *The Georgia Review* in 1968 by a fellow Savannahnian, Alexander A. Lawrence. With numerous quotations from Aiken's work Lawrence points out that Savannah was on the poet's mind throughout his life. Lawrence says that though Aiken considered Savannah to be the city where his youth was destroyed, in which even the number of his parents' house "held his life in its poisonous coils," it was for Aiken always the "miraculous city."[6] The reason for this, I believe, is that it was in Savannah that Aiken experienced the profoundest emotions of his life. Long a distinguished judge in Savannah, Lawrence took a copy of his article to Aiken for his friend to read. Later Lawrence would write Luck F. Gambrell that tears came to Aiken's eyes as he read the article; when he finished it, with all its moving descriptions of Aiken's childhood and his parents' death, he pronounced it entirely true.

---

[5]Conrad Aiken, *Ushant* (Cleveland: The World Publishing Co., 1962), 162. All references in the chapters that follow are to this edition.

[6]Alexander A. Lawrence, "228 Habersham Street," *The Georgia Review* 22 (Fall, 1968), 319.

In my own article in 1972 in *The Southern Review*, called "Conrad Aiken: Resident of Savannah," I have sought to present some of the ordinary aspects of the life of Aiken as part-time resident in the city. Aiken in fact played an important role in the redevelopment of a city long down at heels. In 1960 he convinced Hy Sobiloff, a man often described in the press as a millionaire poet, to visit the city. Sobiloff bought the house adjoining Aiken's old home (now 230 Oglethorpe Avenue but then 228 Habersham Street, as it is called in *Blue Voyage*), and allowed Conrad and his wife Mary to live there rent-free. From 1962 until 1972 the Aikens spent roughly half the year in Savannah and the other in Brewster, Massachusetts, in an inherited house called "Forty-one Doors." By 1972 Aiken's various illnesses, including a painful skin disease called pemphigies, made it impossible for him to go any more to Brewster for the winter. On August 17, 1973, twelve days after his eighty-fourth birthday, he died, and he was buried, as he had carefully provided for, beside his parents in Bonaventure cemetery. But almost to the end Aiken maintained a lively interest in the city, and was credited in the February 7, 1972 issue of *Newsweek* with having first urged the Poetry Society of Georgia, the state's oldest poetry society, located in Savannah, to invite Sobiloff to come to Savannah. This visit, in fact, gave new impetus to the efforts of Historic Savannah Foundation, Inc., to renovate the inner city.

My article showing Aiken's various connections with people of Savannah as well as Robert N. Wilson's reminiscence in the *Harvard Magazine* serve to reveal Aiken in his ordinary moments as a man and a writer. Inevitably his actions and his own work, as well as remarks by fellow writers, have easily led casual literary observers to see Aiken as a withdrawn, even reclusive individual. Malcolm Cowley ends his own reminescence in *The Southern Review* with Aiken's statement in *Ushant* that he early resolved to live "off-stage, behind the scenes, out of view." Cowley concludes that Aiken never wanted literary celebrity by asking: "Was it all part of the same pattern as his resigning from Harvard in preference to writing and publicly reading the class poem?"[7] Clarissa Lorenz in *Lorelei Two* makes it abundantly clear, however, that Aiken often said he wanted to be widely read and that in some ways he was a literary celebrity in America and England between the wars. Aiken, as Cowley suggests, could never bear much public exposure. He told me once that during his year of teaching at Harvard, never

---

[7]Cowley, 258.

completed due to dismissal because of the complaints of several graduates, that he had allowed Nathan Pusey, one of his students and later a Harvard president, in effect to teach a class for him. But to say, as Cowley does, that Aiken hated intruders, is extremely misleading. Wilson in his article, as I do in mine, makes it quite clear how approachable Aiken was and how much he loved conversation on a wide variety of topics. One quotation from Wilson about life at "Forty-one Doors" in Brewster should clarify Aiken's attitude toward people:

> The house was often a harbor for students, whether those on a formal, paying basis, being tutored in poetry or painting, or simply young guests whose ideas the Aikens wished to entertain. In part, I think this was, somewhat deliberately a strategy of Conrad's for staying in touch with the life of his times. But it was never artificial, never a pose, and the poet in his sixties had the essential creative individual's talent for seeming ever youthful, ever poised against the world with a naive curiosity.[8]

Wilson's sense of Aiken in his sixties as a man of youthful creativity is echoed by various people I have talked to who knew him. My own impressions of Aiken in yearly interviews between 1965 and 1969 are that of a personal creativity and an openness to the life around him.

Cowley's article is right to suggest that there were times, all his life, when Aiken did withdraw from everyone to pursue his creative activities as both thinker, reader, and writer. Yet Aiken was capable of both an act of withdrawal and of regular creative relationships with life, including an awareness of stock markets or comic strips or small Savannah shops, facts of life that many poets would find insignificant. Aiken's doctrine of consciousness meant, among other things, the need to be conscious of all life, to be one, as Henry James helped him to see, on whom nothing is lost. Younger poets, in turning away both from a consciousness of ordinary life as well as from those necessary periods of withdrawal, leaned too much on each other, Aiken believed; they "'swap juices' a little too much, so that they are in danger of losing their own identity," Aiken said in his *Paris Review*

---

[8]Robert N. Wilson, "Conrad Aiken: An Appreciation," *Harvard Magazine* 82 (July-August, 1980), 6.

Interview.[9] My own awareness, at the time of first meeting Aiken, concerning the important problem of the creative life, which I discussed in detail with him, I summed up thus in my reminiscence: "Aiken has always managed to be at once active and contemplative. To be both at the same time is a rare and dying art. Literary people are losing this ability, along with everybody else, as Aiken himself has pointed out."[10] Aiken's ability to withdraw for artistic purposes and then to return at regular intervals to ordinary life Cowley fails to take into full account, yet he is also precise in describing an essential shyness Aiken always possessed and a slowness in opening up to others. And, as Cowley points out, Aiken "refused to attend literary dinners and could seldom be inveigled into cocktail parties."[11] Nevertheless, he was an extremely sociable man, as Cowley himself notes.

The importance of the Cowley reminiscence of Aiken lies in its scope. It presents the writer at the beginning of his first great creative period, in 1918, still very much attached to Harvard University even to the point of wearing what Cowley calls the "Harvard uniform of the period: white button-down Oxford shirt and brown suit." Cowley moves on to his final meeting with Aiken in Savannah in 1972, a time when Aiken could talk freely about the literary world, "not so excitedly as at our first meeting half a century before."[12] Then Cowley sums up Aiken's belief in what he had accomplished, his full assurance that, in spite of complaints to Cowley in earlier years concerning his work's neglect, he had made his mark on the significant literature of his day. Thus Cowley ends his article:

> He had done his work and knew it was good. He had proclaimed his religion of consciousness and had lived by its tenets. He had never compromised, and he could feel certain that, for all his hatred of intruders, the great world would some day come round to him.[13]

Cowley's description of Aiken at eighty sums up a view of the man held by those who knew him in his last years in Savannah. This view was that Aiken,

---

[9]*The Paris Review* (Winter/Spring, 1968), 117.
[10]Ted R. Spivey, "Conrad Aiken: Resident of Savannah" *The Southern Review* 8 (Autumn, 1972), 799.
[11]Cowley, 246.
[12]Ibid., 259.
[13]Ibid.

even though he had ceased to write his best work, remained a man filled with the spirit of creativity. This creativity grew out of what Cowley calls the poet's "religion of consciousness." Cowley's article is important for two other reasons. It makes clear Aiken's allegiance to Harvard, and it shows his third wife, the painter Mary Hoover, in her own creative and beneficent light: "[B]ut he still made puns while his beloved wife mixed martinis."[14]

Everyone writing about Aiken who had observed Conrad and Mary together reports the closeness of their relationship and the creativity that grew out of it. Robert Wilson's tribute to Mary Hoover is particularly moving. His knowledge of Aiken's third marriage is important for understanding the man now that his divorced second wife, Clarissa Lorenz, has published her own memoir of their relationship. Lorenz's volume, *Lorelei Two*, reveals much concerning the poet's dark side, a side he freely admits manifested itself at the beginning of his second great creative period in 1931. His overcoming the powers of the shadow are recorded in his poems and fiction of the thirties. In 1937 he divorced his second wife and married Mary Hoover the same year. Inevitably, bitterness would grow out of Aiken's flight from Clarissa to Mary, but the bitterness was greater for Clarissa than for Aiken. The suffering Aiken records in *Great Circle* (1933), which grew out of his first wife's leaving him, was so psychologically wrenching that it was probably necessary for the poet to avoid another such psychological explosion in order to keep his sanity. Clarissa bore the heavier burden of their joint suffering through a ten-year relationship. As a man who clung to particular places, Aiken would return to Boston and Cambridge, as his second marriage disintegrated, to find in that area for the third time, a new wife. Then in a minor work of fiction, *A Heart for the Gods of Mexico,* Aiken recorded in part his own flight with Mary to Cuernevaca, Mexico, to obtain a quick divorce. In Cuernevaca the couple were closely associated with Malcolm Lowry and his wife at the time Lowry was struggling with his novel *Under the Volcano*, part of which records his relationship with the Aikens. What the Mexican sojourn meant in creative terms for Aiken is described in *Ushant*. What the fiction written about this period by both Lowry and Aiken indicates is that, essentially, Aiken as an artist needed a domestic situation in order to pursue his work. For him Boston was the place

---

[14]Ibid.

where a new domesticity had begun after the break-up of the first domesticity of his parents' home.

Cowley, meeting Aiken in Boston in 1918, was immediately impressed with the fact that Aiken "was already the author of two red-haired children and four published volumes of post-romantic poetry."[15] Aiken's new life as husband and father, beginning with his marriage to Jessie McDonald in 1912, was one of his most important steps in rediscovering the loss of his family in 1901. Jessie's importance to him is recorded in *Great Circle* and other works; she clearly played an important role in stimulating his creativity. But Aiken's own unfaithfulness led directly to the breakup of this once fruitful union. Aiken's second marriage ultimately failed during the 1930s because of his own extreme demands on Clarissa, demands growing out of Aiken's powerful suicidal impulses, which put enormous pressure on both him and his wife. That Aiken could recover from his disastrous second marriage to find with Mary Hoover one of the most fruitful marriages an American writer has known in this century, together with the fact that he maintained all his life close connections with his three children, should give the lie to Clarissa's implications that Aiken was, as she put it, a ravager of other people. The second marriage, as I will suggest later, was clearly significant in Aiken's life not only for the fact that Clarissa literally saved him from suicide but that she also lent him strength in what was in the early and middle thirties probably the most difficult and most creative period of his career. It was in this period that he directed his literary efforts toward writing the major philosophical poetry he had early felt called to write. Above all else he prepared himself during the thirties for his masterwork of self-confession, the biography in prose-poetry he would call *Ushant.*

Aiken's first marriage in 1912 came in the year that many literary scholars believed marked the real beginning in America of the modern movement in the arts. His chief book of poetry before this date, *Earth Triumphant,* inspired by John Masefield, he set aside as being unimportant to his development. The book that had impressed Cowley as a junior at Harvard was *The Jig of Forslin* because of, in Cowley's words, "what it had done in the symphonic form."[16] The poems Aiken called the Symphonies would be his chief contribution to a new creative outburst in America that in large part had its beginnings in Boston, New York, and Chicago. When

---

[15]Ibid., 246.
[16]Ibid., 245.

Cowley found himself talking freely with Aiken, after an initial hesitation because of the poet's shyness, a hesitation that many people would feel with him, they were walking through the streets of Boston. They had discovered that they "both liked Boston in decay," had "notions about the French symbolists," and were interested in "achieving architectural and musical effects in verses such as Aiken in fact had achieved." Cowley then goes on: "Soon we were talking without pauses, talking with such excitement--at least on my part--that I didn't notice the streets through which we wandered before parting at the door of Aiken's house on the unfashionable side of Beacon Hill."[17] In the late sixties I would in my own meetings with Aiken find an initial hesitation on the poet's part to begin conversation, followed by an intensity of interest in discussing literature unmatched in anyone I have ever met. The Aiken passion for walking through city streets continued into his late seventies as the poet daily walked in Savannah, closely observing old buildings. At the end of most days in Savannah he and Mary would walk from their house to the Savannah River, carrying with them a thermos of martinis.

Although Boston itself was a central fact in Aiken's early life as a man and an artist, Cambridge, I believe, was the only city that equalled Savannah in its influence on the poet. This was primarily because of Harvard, the place where Aiken encountered the two men probably most important to his creative development--George Santayana and T. S. Eliot. What these two men meant to him as man and artist will be discussed in two separate chapters. What Harvard meant to him can be seen in Cowley's reminiscence; it was a place where art and philosophy could be freely discussed. Aiken's first awareness of art in all its joys and sorrows occurred in Savannah. The second great movement of poetic and philosophic awareness for the poet came at Harvard. That Aiken all his life continued to draw sustenance from his alma mater can be seen clearly in Wilson's reminiscence about the poet's life in the forties. Part of Aiken's mind and heart always seemed to dwell there. When I talked literature and philosophy with him it was still Santayana and Eliot he mentioned the most. People were always more important than anything else but places were also very important.

New England itself was one great setting for Aiken, and in the final phase of his art he delved into his family history in a region that had its

---

[17]Ibid., 246.

beginnings not as an extension of Europe, as in the Southern colonies, but as a new political entity, still, he believed, awaiting its ultimate discovery by poets and philosophers. Yet Aiken cannot be called a New England poet as Robert Frost, for instance, can be. When he left Savannah to live first in New Bedford and then in Cambridge, Aiken experienced a continuation of that family trauma he had known in Savannah. But in place of the growing insanity of his father and the hysteria of his mother, he knew isolation, loneliness, and even ostracism because of his family tragedy. Ironically, when he would go to preparatory school in Concord, he would sense little of that spirit of Transcendentalism that would later play a large role in his philosophy and poetry. But Transcendentalism, which later came to him through his grandfather's work, was far from his mind in the village of Emerson, Thoreau, and Hawthorne. It was not that village of Concord, whre Transcendentalism once flourished, that drew Aiken's attention but rather the great cities of the beginnings of a new trans-Atlantic literature, among them Boston, New York, London. Later still, he was attracted to the reviving cities of Spain. Largely through his awareness of this new creativity, Aiken was gradually able to overcome his early painful isolation.

Harvard, as a university that has often alienated mavericks like Aiken, ironically meant liberation from that New England that Aiken as a teenager had experienced. It was the first great liberation of his life when he discovered James and Santayana, who had made Harvard's Department of Philosophy world famous. Furthermore, Harvard pointed Aiken toward Europe. In the first decade of this century Harvard was not the educational bastion of a nation confident in its world leadership. Instead, the leaders of new thought at Harvard felt it was their duty to awaken a puritanical and culturally stagnant America to new forms of thought and art then fermenting on both sides of the Atlantic, with Europe seeming then far more culturally developed than the United States. Aiken, Walter Lippmann, T. S. Eliot, and others studied under Santayana, who was himself soon to leave for Europe. In his biography of Lippmann, D. Steven Blum says that the man who was to become America's foremost journalist wanted "to awaken the United States to new dimensions of existence. This motif was of the utmost significance to him, and to many like minded members of his generation."[18]

The great American exile movement was thus coming into its own even while Aiken was at Harvard. Its aim was in part to get away from a

---

[18]D. Steven Blum, *Walter Lippmann* (Ithaca: Cornell University Press, 1984), 39.

provincial America, but it also sought to improve the American arts and American thought and thereby lift the whole nation out of a self-imposed isolation. Thus Aiken would in 1930 write from England to Theodore Spencer, one of a growing number of Americans beginning to doubt the wisdom of American writers continuing to be exiles: "Pour moi, America is a weariness of the flesh and spirit" and "Not that I don't like America. I like it if anything too much."[19] Aiken was always something of a New England Transcendentalist, and this side of him grew stronger as he grew older, but he never really plunged into New England to find the main subject of his art until late in life in works that are part of his coda. For one reason, his early literary and intellectual masters did not take him in the direction of New England. Cowley says that "his intellectual masters had been Poe first of all, then Santayana, Freud and Henry James."[20] Besides, he personally had little in common with the New England lifestyle of the early twentieth century. Cowley continues: "He would have been out of place in Emerson's Concord, since he continued all his life to be fond of women, mischief, bawdy limericks, and martinis.

Nevertheless, at the end of his long career, he had worked round to a position reminiscent of that which Emerson had reached in 1831, before he had published anything."[21] But unlike Emerson, Aiken never revolted against Harvard or any other aspect of organized higher education, inspite of the fact that Harvard had dismissed him as a guest lecturer before his contract had expired. He once admitted to me that his innate shyness had always made him a poor teacher, and that he probably deserved to be dismissed. Yet as a literary tutor to Malcolm Lowry and several other younger writers he was brilliant.

Cambridge was the essential city in his Northeastern experience because there Harvard was, the place where his intellectual development had begun as a student and where he first found people of like mind who would encourage him in his literary and philosophical aspirations. I can remember Aiken in his seventies talking of Harvard as if he had been a student there

---

[19]*Selected Letters of Conrad Aiken*, ed. Joseph Killorin (New Haven: Yale University Press, 1978), 160.
[20]Cowley, 257.
[21]Ibid.

only recently. He was still upset that his university had deserted its Unitarian heritage to become Episcopalian in orientation.

Cowley believes that something like Emerson's philosophy was where Aiken ended his career, yet his last book-length poem, *Thee*, presents a view of transcendence not found in Emerson. Late poems like "A Letter from Li Po" and "The Crystal" present a vision of the interconnection between language and landscape and, as in the latter poem, an exploration of the world from the viewpoint of the Pythagorean theory of number as the key to the reality of the cosmos. Cowley's understanding of Aiken's views in old age is, of course, limited. To claim that Aiken speaks with a New England voice, as Cowley does, is to ignore the many voices of Aiken, which he continued to speak with until the end of his life, as Joseph Killorin points out often in his edition of the poet's letters. Even in his speaking Aiken expressed his absorption of the ways of life found in three areas: the coastal South, Cambridge, Massachusetts, and southern England. Thus Robert N. Wilson speaks of his voice as he remembers hearing it at Harvard in 1949: "His voice was soft, beautifully modulated, not quite pure Harvard or the Savannah of his youth or the England he so loved, but something of all three."[22] Yet he could also project his imagination into cultures as diverse as those of Spain, of China, and of Mexico. He was always a writer who involved himself with the spirit of place, and it is not surprising that living in Savannah in his old age he should, in his own deeply individualistic way, write a poem addressing a transcendent God. Religion in the South has always put more emphasis on transcendence than on immanence. And yet in "The Poet in Granada" he could capture the essence of both Roman Catholic ritual and the Spanish bullfight. This poem, often neglected, is one of his most important works; it is also a poem whose value Aiken in old age greatly appreciated, as he in fact told me on several occasions.

Killorin in his introduction to the letters is right to emphasize the line from "A Letter from Li Po" that stresses the idea of the word being related to the landscape: "The landscape and the language are the same."[23] Like other poets working in the symbolist tradition, Aiken often links poetry and place. The greatest symbolists writing in English -- Yeats, Eliot, Stevens, Pound, Auden -- all make much of the spirit of place. Like the Romantics before them, those Anglo-American poets who are identified with the

---

[22]Wilson, 6.
[23]*Selected Letters*, 20.

international movement called symbolism were deeply concerned with the human spirit, but, being affected by the earlier movement of realism, they sought in their identification with particular places to avoid the excessive Romantic concern with a disembodied spirituality. As D. H. Lawrence said of Whitman, who had one foot in Romanticism and the other in realism, he put the soul down among the potsherds. Aiken was self-consciously very much a part of this movement to locate the human spirit in the particular places of his varied intense experiences on two continents. But ever the mediator, Aiken would seek to maintain the Romantic belief that through recollection one could bring to the artwork an experience of infinity. In his search for recollection Aiken plays the role of a modern shaman who can recall, like earlier shamans, moments paradisiac in nature. Killorin has linked this shamanic ability, in part at least, to certain ecstatic moments in the poet's Savannah childhood. Thus he quotes Aiken concerning what the poet called "that most magical of cities": "I was to run wild in that earthly paradise till I was nine--no school till nine... I can still remember that feeling every morning of having before one an infinity of freedom."[24] Aiken scholars often begin their work with his most powerful early memory: the tragic murder-suicide of his parents. To approach Aiken as both Romantic and symbolist one should put beside that memory the other powerful memories of an early intuition of paradise and immortality. To do so is to understand both the symbolist's awareness of suffering and the Wordsworthian belief that the child is essentially the human being's father, which is to say the childhood experience of infinity forms the basis of adult life. To recall the childhood awareness of paradise is thus to capture what Aiken calls in "Tetélestai" the "secret of self." But Aiken did not make the Romantic mistake of trying to seize infinity. As a modern symbolist he knew that the awareness of paradise could only happen occasionally; nevertheless, the search for this awareness was for Aiken the central act of his life. As a modernist Aiken also rejected the intense individualism of Romantics like Wordsworth, Keats, Shelley, Melville, Emerson, and others who also influenced him. The isolated loneliness we see in the older Emerson or Melville was not for Aiken. Even Eliot and Stevens seem isolated when compared with Aiken, who in his life and work always reached out to communal associations. In his association with literary comrades and in his

---

[24]Ibid., 4.

love for several women Aiken forged a poetry of brotherhood almost unique in his century, one largely ignored, still waiting to be discovered in all its depth.

Chapter 3

Literary Comrades and Perilous Lovers

Conrad Aiken carefully spelled out the meaning, for him, of certain specific places, so much so that evidence of his various attachments to Savannah, New York, Cambridge, Rye, and London opens the door to arguments about what place he most truly belonged to. The answer must be to no one place because, as Aiken makes clear early in *Ushant*, uprootedness, not attachment to places, is modern man's most basic condition: "And here too, at the very beginning, was the principle of *uprootedness* that especially now, at the end of the great war, seemed so terribly to govern all lives (*Ushant*, 20)." Yet throughout *Ushant* Aiken the mediator must continually present scenes and emotions from specific places. He must weigh the culture of the South against that of New England; he must imaginatively hold America and Europe in the balance, never rejecting one or the other.

The chief reason is that, more than most modern poets, Aiken retained his attachment to Romanticism, particularly the Wordsworthian branch of the movement, but also he held to branches represented by Keats and Shelley. Wordsworth counselled that the child is father to the man and that poetry is emotion recollected in tranquility. To follow these poetic prescriptions Aiken found it always necessary to return in memory to childhood scenes and to hold in that memory all the great emotional experiences of his life. With the New England Transcendentalists and with Wordsworth, Keats, and Shelley he would seek divine impulses from continuing encounters with nature. Yet, though always mediating between Romanticism and symbolism, Aiken as poet and man of letters was primarily a symbolist, though, as I will eventually show, he was a symbolist in the process of becoming a surrealist.

Even though he was an influential critic and literary theorist, Aiken never fully defined the symbolist movement in literature. With Pound, Eliot, Fletcher, Stevens, Williams, and other poets he studied the characteristics of modern poetry and often sought to pinpoint many aspects of the modernist impulse, of which symbolism was only one aspect, though probably the most important aspect. Like the twentieth-century followers of Baudelaire and Mallarmé, who are often credited with launching the symbolist movement, Aiken accepted the view of modern man as being an individual uprooted from his dying cultural traditions, existing primarily in an urban environment. Baudelaire had thought of himself as a Romantic writing under the influence of Poe. The city was, Baudelaire believed, the one great subject left for the Romantic. When he began to write about his own city, Paris, Baudelaire described, often in religious terms, the various neuroses of modern city dwellers in his one great book, *Flowers of Evil*. Aiken would accept the neuroses and suffering of modern man as a starting point for much of his best work, but in one important way he would differ from the great French poets of the modernist tradition: for human beings in the modern city to survive, Aiken believed, they must have comrades as well as lovers. They must expect to suffer at the hands of both comrades and lovers, but they should not, as so many of the poets of the Decadence and of Aestheticism did, withdraw into ivory towers or into alcohol or into the Church or into any one aspect of life. To survive in the alienated and alienating urban scene that had become the twentieth-century world one must, Aiken believed, accept the help of others and one must have some kind of calling. There is more of Whitman in Aiken than meets the eye, but the great Whitmanesque embracing of everyone is not for Aiken; yet a few companions necessary to one's calling, Aiken believed, should be met on something like Whitman's open road and necessarily embraced.

Speaking of the comrades he had met, Aiken states in *Ushant*: "[H]e was now as much these as himself, they and those others who still lived, the friends, were himself" (*Ushant*, 14). After acknowleging the fact that the "men were oneself, Aiken defines the role of the women also encountered on the journey: "[T]he women, no matter how deeply loved, nor with what all-givingness or agony or ecstasy, were not; they paralleled, they accompanied, they counterpointed, but they did not, in the same sense, become intimately the alphabet one one's soul" (*Ushant*, 14). Like Whitman, Aiken believed that the encounter with comrades was necessary as part of both the development of the soul and development of the poet's art, and he saw the two as closely related. He believed that his encounters with women, who were always perilous in a way that men could not be, were necessary for both psychic and poetic development, but neither in *Ushant* nor in his other work does he explain in detail this necessity. There are no great love poems in Aiken's work, like those in the work of Yeats, and no memorable female characters in his fiction.

Nevertheless, his work reveals more about various aspects of male-female relationships than that of most American authors. To put figures who influenced Aiken--Emerson, Melville, Whitman, Poe, Dickinson, Eliot, Robinson, Pound, Stevens--alongside the poet will help a reader to understand how much Aiken struggled to understand the opposite sex and how much he contributed to the most neglected theme in American literature, which is surely gender relationships. Leslie Fiedler is doubtlessly correct, as he tells us in *Love and Death in the New American Novel*, that most great American writers fail to take women into account as people in their work. Henry James is one great exception. Aiken admired James long before he became fashionable with critics, chiefly because of that author's highly developed consciousness and because he did present women as fully developed individuals. But as an artist Aiken's development was largely carried on through interaction with male comrades.

Aiken began his real literary career in a communal manner as a member of the *Advocate* staff at Harvard, working with his lifelong friend, T. S. Eliot. Out of his association with Eliot and later with other poets like Ezra Pound and William Carlos Williams, he developed the kind of modern awareness that James in his fiction would in time make famous. Jamesian awareness was not really different from the kind cultivated by the new symbolist poets that Arthur Symons wrote about in *The Symbolist Movement in Literature* (1899), the book that Eliot credited with launching his own serious poetic efforts.

From reading Symons, Eliot was directed to a serious consideration of Mallarmé and other French symbolists; from this study came a poetic experimentation that led in time to "The Love Song of J. Alfred Prufrock," the work that William York Tindall believed to be the first truly symbolist poem written in English. Symons, on the other hand, recognized Yeats as the first English poet to be a symbolist, though most critics today would call Yeats's early poems that Symons admired examples of literary impressionism. What Yeats, Symons, and other poets had in common was their complicated modern sensibility that was indeed partly a product of the new symbolist awareness, which involved a complexity and a concern with myths and ideas largely rejected by the materialistic, increasingly work-oriented civilization surrounding them everywhere. The symbol would in fact become the central and necessary device for combatting the realists, who dominated literature at the turn of the century.

Symons's book was in part a call to a small group of like-minded individuals, all men, to unite in order to work together for what was believed to be the beginning of a new literary movement. Eliot and Aiken, even before they had graduated from Harvard, were forming what amounted to a symbolist group. The influence of Santayana, who understood something of this new complicated awareness found in both literary impressionism and in symbolism, served as a guide for Aiken and, to a lesser extent, for Eliot, though Eliot never admitted Santayana's influence. What Santayana taught both poets in the lectures that went into his book *Three Philosophical Poets* was the possibility of a new philosophical poetry. After all, Poe and Baudelaire had availed themselves of philosophy, and Mallarmé and his followers had used philosophy in their poetry. If anything distinguished the new poetry of symbolism other than acute awareness and a refined sensibility, it is the difficult uses made of both philosophy and mythology by symbolists. Both Eliot and Aiken were early concerned with a poetry that recorded philosophical thought as well as feeling, yet, as symbolists, their work differed in many ways.

Eliot was, in fact, one kind of symbolist and Aiken another. Yet the best poetry of both men has in common the characteristics of symbolism described above; nevertheless most definitions of the movement miss what was essential to their work, a sense of brotherhood among poets holding similar views. Anna Balakian in her seminal work *The Symbolist Movement* speaks of "The Symbolists and their international coterie" and thus pinpoints the aims of what amounted to a kind of loose-knit brotherhood that had set itself against all nationalistic literature: "The artistic vision, freed from national ideals, focused on the relationship between the subjective, purely personal world of the artist, and its objective projection."[1] Balakian also shows the relationship between the earlier Romantic movement and surrealism, which moved beyond the symbolists:

A book on Romanticism will tell us that the true Romanticist found his vista in the dream, as the intermediary stage between this world and the next, but so did the symbolist cultivate dreams as the only vital level of existence of the poet, and the surrealist probed the dream world not merely to enjoy the state but thereby to cultivate the possibilities of his mind. The same cult--but for different reasons! The Romanticist aspired to the infinite, the symbolist thought he could discover it, the surrealist believed he could create it; thus the word 'infinite' meant something different to each.[2]

Where Eliot and Aiken most differed was in Aiken's continuing acceptance of both Romanticism and certain viewpoints, connected with mental cultivation, that are in effect surrealist.

---

[1] Anna Balakian, *The Symbolist Movement* (New York: Random House, 1967), 10, 11.
[2] Ibid., 16.

The Eliot-Aiken relationship is so important that it deserves a chapter unto itself because of the many similarities between the two friends. What is possibly even more important for literature than their continuing personal relationship from the time when they served at Harvard as coeditors of the *Advocate* until Eliot's death in 1965 is their continuing concern for the redefinition of literary criticism to achieve the means to appraise the new modernist poetry. This continuing activity was related to the comradeship of the two--which was sometimes painful--and resulted, among other important events, in the launching of Eliot as a symbolist poet. In *The Paris Review* Eliot describes this launching:

> Aiken was a very generous friend. He tried to place some of my poems in London one summer when he was over, with Harold Monroe and others. Nobody would think of publishing them. He brought them back to me. Then in 1914, I think, we were both in London in the summer. He said, "You go to Pound. Show him your poems." He thought Pound might like them. Aiken liked them, though they were different from his.[3]

Pound, of course, pronounced the poems truly modernist and Eliot was thus launched as a poet. Aiken's generosity should be noted here because (as Clarissa Lorenz often demonstrated) Aiken in literary and other affairs could be irascible. Yet the generosity that Eliot describes would be a recurring aspect of Aiken's role as a literary comrade. In 1931 Aiken had already recognized Wallace Stevens as one of the great modern poets. Thus he wrote R. P. Blackmur: "Eliot will go *down* somewhat (keeping however a marked historical importance, in addition to his pure merit) and Stevens will, I feel sure, come up."[4] How right, of course, time has proved this judgment. In 1931 and later, Stevens had received no real critical or popular consideration, and Aiken's continued support led Stevens, somewhat incorrectly considering how acerbic and even arrogant Aiken could sometimes be, to write: "He seems to be entirely without selfishness and aggressiveness. . . he is honest, unaffected and a man of general all-round integrity."[5] Like Pound when promoting the work of the best modernist writers, Aiken could rise

---

[3] *Writers at Work: The Paris Review Interviews*, Second Series (New York: The Viking Press, 1963), 95.
[4] *Selected Letters of Conrad Aiken*, ed. Joseph Killorin (New Haven: Yale University Press, 1978), 170.
[5] Ibid., 337.

above selfishness and pettiness. The two men are probably the most important evaluative critics in the whole movement of Anglo-American symbolism, if not in all of modern literature in English. Personal generosity was an important aspect of both men. Both would, as Eliot says of Aiken, accept and promote work different from their own without letting personal friendship affect their own literary judgment. For instance, in 1913, Aiken was attacking Pound in an unpublished letter to the editor of *Poetry* for his nationalism in putting the new poetry of America far above modernist poetry in Britain, which Aiken was familiar with in detail: "Really, Mr. Pound becomes at times autocratic, high-handed. He writes good poetry, when he is not too intent upon writing good poetry, for which I am one among many who are grateful."[6] Aiken was, as usual, correct in his judgments of Pound, who would himself shortly give up his nationalistic stance and accept an international view of modernist literature very similar to Aiken's. After 1913 Pound would join the great symbolist poets and novelists like Eliot, Yeats, Joyce, Aiken, Rilke, Stevens, and many others in a movement that, according to Balakian, "reaches its apogee around 1920, despite new movements that pull in opposite directions the literary talents of the new century." Describing the central importance of this movement, Balakian goes on to say:

> In fact, the success and the large-scale ramification and popularization in poetic circles of the symbolist technique and spirit are made glaringly evident by the fact that every poet honored with the Nobel Prize, from the time of Maeterlinck, carries to a larger degree the character and conventions of symbolism than any other distinctive feature: Jimenez, St. John Perse, and Quasimodo have this common family trait. The hermetic character of symbolism became a universal code.[7]

For Balakian the important names in symbolism (she uses a small "s" for the European as opposed to the French aspect of the movement) at the moment of apogee in 1920 are Eliot, Valéry, Perse, Jimenez, Betti, Stevens, Rilke, and Yeats. Yet, as Balakian suggests, other poets not as completely committed to the movement as these figures combine elements from other movements. Among these must be placed Pound and Aiken, who, in spite of their continuing internationalism, also remained with one foot in the nationalistic camp while often denying their connections with it. Pound never

---

[6]Ibid., 22.
[7]*The Symbolist Movement*, 158.

fully lost his belief that Whitman was a great American bard, a teacher of modern man. Pound and Aiken were both teachers as well as poets and men of letters. Thus Aiken in *Ushant* lists Pound as one of his literary comrades under the name Rabbi Ben Ezra. This title is partly a smack at Ezra's anti-Semitism, which Aiken detested for many reasons, one of them being that he sometimes saw himself as a kind of Leopold Bloom wandering through the world rejected and sexually frustrated. The name also is a compliment to Pound for his attempt to achieve a ripe wisdom of age along with his significant literary expression. Aiken would emulate Pound's efforts to achieve the ripe wisdom of advanced years, and, in fact, so would Eliot. In *Ushant* and his mature verse Aiken would reveal his own ripe wisdom of advancing age, suggesting often, as Browning's Rabbi Ben Ezra did, that the best of life is old age. Ironically, Pound after 1930 seemed to move from the course he set himself, becoming in the thirties and forties a kind of American crank, but it was the Pound that Aiken knew before 1920 that inspired him with thoughts of gaining the wisdom found in age.

After 1920 Aiken failed to maintain his personal relationship with Pound, yet he continued to be Santayana's friend; and it was this relationship more than any other that helped him to believe that philosophical poetry was still possible. The nationalistic impulse that Aiken had seen at work in Pound was linked to a deeper belief about poetry that Aiken shared with many modern poets in America: there must be, he thought, a movement beyond the formalism of an Eliot, beyond a formalism Aiken himself prized, in order to record poetically experiences found in what Pound would call "the green world." Linked with this search for "greeness," found also in Lorca, who was greatly admired by Aiken, is the need to interpret America in its wholeness. After completing the Preludes, which are among his best symbolist poems, Aiken in *A Heart for the Gods of Mexico* and *The Kid* would turn to attempts to interpret America in its totality. But the elements of Whitman probably strongest in Aiken are his continuing awareness of himself and his own self-development and his exaltation of the relationship with comrades. Richard Ellmann and Robert O'Clair in their introduction to Whitman in *The Norton Anthology of Modern Poetry* sum up an aspect of this poet that reminds us greatly of Aiken: "his pretense of telling all while leaving much to be gathered, his reckless assumption that the poet, his language, his subject matter, and his readers are all part of one expanding community."[8]

---

[8] *The Norton Anthology of Modern Poetry* eds. Richard Ellmann and Robert O'Clair (New York: W. W. Norton & Co., 1973), 14.

Aiken lacks the expansive self-consciousness of Whitman and is far more deeply aware of the burden of chaos everyone carries in the modern world, but in spite of being a symbolist in much of his best work Aiken could never accept the formalist demands of Eliot and others, and he could never separate his poetry from the life of the past or from the lives of his friends. Underlying *Ushant*, however, is the same assumption one finds in Whitman: to have touched my poetry is to have touched a man.

Aiken for many reasons, his concern with death and psychic pain being chief among them, could not accept much in Whitman's transcendentalist vision. Thus he hardly ever mentions Whitman in his criticism. Aiken tended to reject any kind of Romanticism that seemed to him to be pretentious. For instance, once when I asked him what he thought of Yeats, Aiken showed no enthusiasm at all for him and only mentioned what he believed was a certain pretentiousness in the Irish poet's character. Always in Aiken there was a bedrock honesty and a personal caution. There was also possibly a hidden reason for Aiken's not becoming involved with Whitman's work. Lorenz speaks of Aiken's fear of homosexuality, and much of his early poetry reveals sexual uneasiness and a need to establish a sexual role for himself. Yet what probably links Aiken in an underground way to Whitman is the Quaker background of both. The sense of an inner light given to everyone and the necessity of a human being to be truly oneself, is strong in both poets. Therefore the real comrades for both poets are those who are seeking to find and express that inner light, or that imaginative vision, necessary for the kind of rich consciousness Aiken believed the human race was striving to achieve. Whitman and Aiken, possibly because of their Quaker and Unitarian backgrounds, remained more deeply Transcendentalist than most Americans, though Aiken's Transcendentalism is expressed in a far different, less ebullient manner from Whitman's.

For Balakian the great link between Romanticism and symbolism is Swedenborg's concept of correspondences, an idea that is deeply embedded in the work of both Whitman and Baudelaire. The concept, as stated by Balakian, is that "every natural, physical vision had its penumbra of spiritual recognition."[9] That is, through nature we can apprehend a divine realm if our imaginations are properly attuned to this realm. For poets like Whitman, Emerson, and Aiken who firmly held to this idea inherited through the Quaker-Swedenborgian-Unitarian traditions, comradeship is far more than a friendship based on literary interests held in common, though this link

---

[9]*The Symbolist Movement*, 13.

between people is also deeply honored. Everyone is potentially a comrade because all bear the divine imprint, but the deepest comradeship exists between those who are fully devoted to the task of purifying the imagination and achieving a richer consciousness. But for Aiken and the other modern symbolists, Poe and Baudelaire and their followers point to the necessity of making many plunges into the pools of chaos. Only by taking death and psychic disintegration into consideration could the process leading both to imaginative development and a ripe wisdom of old age ever be attained.

Many of the symbolists, following Baudelaire's plunge into the modern psychosexual chaos, fell into deep pessimism. Continental symbolism often became so concerned with death that the drive toward expanded consciousness would come to a halt for most poets in the movement. Yet one modern French symbolist, in particular, found his way back to the Swedenborgian path Baudelaire had tried to follow. Perse, Balakian tells us, "shed the 'decadent' spirit inherent in early symbolism, while retaining the verbal and metaphoric techniques."[10] The same is also true of Aiken, whose early Symphonies, which take into account the poet's psychosexual entanglements, contain authentic aspects of modern decadence. But like Jimenez and Yeats, Perse uses images of the sea to suggest, in Balakian's words, "the voyage of the soul." Finally, in Perse, Balakian states that "We detect a return, full circle, to a more authentic Swendenborgian assurance of the correspondence of Heaven and Earth."[11]

That Perse and Aiken were both moving on similar voyages of the soul leading to new Swedenborgian assurances can be seen in the great tribute Perse paid Aiken by attending a performance of his play *Mr. Arcularis* at Cape Cod in 1949. In 1950 Aiken reported to Edward Burra that Perse at a cocktail party had said that "'alone in America' he [Aiken] practiced the whole art of poetry, combining the classic with the modern, and with a sense of narrative and composition!"[12] Perse, who also for a short time resided in Savannah writing poetry, had picked Aiken as the one American symbolist who could still affirm life in the midst of modern decadence, his own included, because he continued the voyage of the soul.

Symbols of water are central to some of the best work of Yeats, Eliot, Perse, Stevens, Jimenez, and Aiken because they were symbolists who, though often differing in their approaches to life and to art, had raised their

---

[10]Ibid., 191.

[11]Ibid., 192.

[12]*Selected Letters of Conrad Aiken*, 289.

awareness of the fructifying power of life represented by water, one of the world's chief ritual symbols of psychic renewal. In Eliot's *Quartets* and Aiken's Preludes water and the voyage of the soul suggest how, working through different spiritual traditions, the two friends were able to continue their own development of consciousness into a ripe wisdom that their earlier friend Pound never achieved.

In *Ushant* Aiken's one poetic friend who, in spite of their many differences, remained with him into old age was Eliot. Yet two other friends who cracked up along the way--John Gould Fletcher and Malcolm Lowry--were nearly as important. Lowry and Nita, his girlfriend, were central to the most important vision in all of Aiken's work, the dream of the voyage on which much of *Ushant* is based. For some readers the Aiken autobiography is chiefly about the poet's many literary associations; but, as important for the history of modern literture as this aspect of the book is, *Ushant* must primarily be seen as a record of the psychic voyage of comrades. The word *Ushant* itself is taken by Aiken from an island, *Ile d'Ouessant*, which is on the route of ship bringing Aiken, his wife, Clarissa, Lowry, and his girlfriend Nita back from a trip to Spain in 1931. Passing the island is dangerous, and Aiken actually awakens from the key dream concerning his life's voyage as the ship passes the dangerous shoals:

> To begin with, of course, D., waking from a dream, in the upper berth of the P & O ship many years before, a ship that was perhaps in difficulties as it turned north towards the dangerous shoals south of *Ile d'Ouessant*, *Ushant*--he had heard the alarm signals, or something of that nature, while still in the dream; there, by the dream mechanism, they had been translated into bell-sounds, but bell-sounds of another meaning. (*Ushant*, 29).

The other meaning is that of the bells in a town Aiken is dreaming of, where a figure called the Teacher from the West is requiring Aiken, Lowry, and Nita to translate a book from German in a series of lessons. By the end of *Ushant* the meaning of the dream has finally been made clear to Aiken concerning his own and the lives of his friends. The dream and its circumstances deeply appealed to Aiken, who here is the symbolist believing he can "discover" glimpses of the infinite instead of identifying with it in the manner of a Romanticist like Whitman.

Yet Aiken is both Romanticist and symbolist in accepting the centrality of certain dreams in his life's pilgramage, or voyage. As Balakian says, "the true Romanticist found his vista in the dream, as the intermediary stage between this world and the next."[13] But for Aiken as modernist the ordinariness of this world is emphasized as in effect an environment for a night vision that puzzles and yet also clarifies. The puzzle is greater than the clarification and its meaning must be sought for years, being revealed through the events of the author's life. Inevitably, Aiken would use the genre of autobiography to describe the dream and both the voyage of 1931 and its connection with his spirit's voyage past dangerous shoals that say "you shall not pass" but that must be passed if the home port is to be made by the voyager.

For Aiken the rationale of autobiography is that, as in some of his best poems and stories, life and literature must be seen as essentially the same. To touch the work is to touch the man even with all his artifices and his tortured paths of memory, at times deceiving even while illuminating what is essential to the human spirit itself. But more of this in a later chapter on *Ushant.*

What the central dream of *Ushant* does clarify is the Aiken-Lowry relationship. In the dream, Hans, who is Lowry, says: "'We are brothers'": next, "'We are son and father'"; and lastly, "'No, we are rivals!'" But even in rivalry maintaining their superiority to . . . woman" (*Ushant*, 29). Lowry and Aiken were deeply drawn to each other as brothers, but Lowry also became Aiken's lawfully adopted son. Their rivalry would, in fact, lead to physical combat, among other things; yet, at the same time, they were united, even chauvinistically, as Clarissa Lorenz maintains in her memoir, in standing above women, whom they were often moved to court with the ardency of an earlier age.

The meaning, however, of the Aiken-Lowry relationship would have to be understood for both men in terms of their lived experience. The dream only provided insights, one of them being that Lowry in Spain revealed a Hamlet quality that portended his gradual disintegration from alcoholism. Yet the dream does not center on the destructive side of Lowry's life but points toward that genius in him that Aiken always knew he had. The meaning of their continuing relationship, particularly as it culminated in their close association in Mexico in the late thirties, is that genius is not something possessed by a single individual. Rather Aiken shows later in *Ushant* that the geniuses within the two men were nourished by their continuing association. Even though Lowry was moving toward personal disintegration, with the

---

[13] *The Symbolist Movement*, 16.

help of Aiken and the destructive Nita, who became his wife, he would write one of the great novels of the century, *Under the Volcano*, a work in which Aiken himself is, as the protagonist's brother, an important character. What Lowry is saying in the novel about male comradeship parallels Aiken's own insights into the subject: true comrades are doubles.

The theme of the double is found in two of Eliot's plays, *The Cocktail Party* and *The Elder Statesman*. If one cannot acknowledge the double, or secret sharer as Joseph Conrad calls this figure in one of his stories, then he cannot understand the roots of his own creativity. No human being, Aiken and Eliot both tell us, can create alone; some form of community is always essential not only for the literary act but also for the movement of the human spirit toward its fulfillment. Whitman had announced in his poetry a new day of comradeship involving men and women on an open road leading to spiritual fulfillment, but that other forerunner of poetic modernism in the eighteen-fifties, Baudelaire, revealed fully in his *Fleur de Mal* a modern urban scene of psychosexual pain and struggle that portended the death of civilization.

While retaining always a degree of Whitman's Transcendental idealism, Aiken is, as a symbolist, in Baudelaire's camp in his depiction of psychic pain. But like Baudelaire, in a few of his poems he suggests the possibility of pushing on through psychosexual agony while acknowledging, like Freud, Aiken's chief mentor on the subject, that all psychic problems have a sexual counterpart and that this sexual counterpart must be acknowledged. In his Symphonies and in *Great Circle*, which Freud kept in his waiting room for his patients to read, Aiken goes into greater detail concerning his own sexual dysfunction than possibly any other modern American writer. Much more work needs to be done in this area of Aiken studies, but the summing up of the Aiken problem goes back, more than anything else, to an unresolved Oedipus complex, as one important dream in *Great Circle* shows. For this reason primarily Aiken refers to his three wives as the three Lorelei and to his lovers as the little Lorelei. Women for Aiken were often seen as sexual sirens luring men to death, but because he was able to break through his Oedipal bonds, Aiken was not permanently bound to a vision of woman as mythic monster.

In *Ushant*, Aiken's regular use of the term Lorelei is often playful, as if to suggest that he had indeed overcome many of those fixations and obsessions recorded in early works like *Priapus and the Pool*. Aiken follows Freud and later psychologists in revealing that behind both the Oedipus complex and Adler's Inferiority complex, which the poet accepted as correct theories based on knowledge demonstrated by the new science of psychology, was the deeper problem of narcissism. Narcissism often caused Aiken to project his own negativism upon women. Only expanded consciousness, he finally realized, could overcome this narcissism. Thus as the poet continues to face the perilous aspect of women, he would seek a large vision, an expanded consciousness, that would enable him to be at last reconciled with all of woman, including her Lorelei aspect.

Aiken's struggle to achieve that expanded consciousness needed for psychic liberation involved not one but several perilous journeys. Fortunately we have the woman's account of his journey of ten years with the most perilous of all his lovers and wives. One probably must discount at least a few of Lorenz's reconstructed conversations in *Lorelei Two*, and one must always allow for her admitted obtuseness in trying to understand Aiken's career as poet and philosopher. She acknowledges, even proudly, quoting others to prove it, that he was both poet and philosopher in an age that had little use for either. Nevertheless, her descriptions of Aiken's rage and cruelty ring true. His awareness of his death wish is strong after their marriage, and, of couse, Aiken owed his life to her for saving him from suicide.

What Lorenz does identify as Aiken's chief problem in his years with her between 1926 and 1936 is his inferiority complex. As Mary Martin Rountree has shown, Aiken in this period was suffering the agonies of middle-aged failure. In spite of some doubts about his sexuality, he had achieved something of that full sexuality that Freud believed was the proper outcome of the psychoanalytic journey. Lorenz notes several times the deep sexual attraction the two had for each other, and she makes it clear that frequent sexual intercourse was an important part of their marriage. But for Lorenz, who was a feminist and a career woman, Aiken's male chauvinism was the chief problem in the marriage. What Lorenz never perceived very clearly was that this chauvinism was largely a result of the poet's sense of failure as a man of letters and that behind this sense of failure lay his father's castrating powers, the early loss of his family, and his rejection as a youth in New England because of his Savannah past.

Looked at from Lorenz's viewpoint throughout much of her book, the marriage was a disaster for both partners in that Aiken seemed to disintegrate to the point of extreme depression, leading to strong suicidal impulses, and Lorenz herself in her painful frustration was continually being plunged into a deepening rage against Aiken's attitude toward her to the point that, before their marriage finally broke apart, she too was considering suicide. Yet in places in her book and finally at the end of it, Lorenz shows an awareness that the whole painful process of her marriage to Aiken was part of a joint creativity that would, through great pain, bring forth new life and work in both her and Aiken. Thus she can end her book:

> We all wish to be remembered for something. In the opinion of critics and familiars like John Aiken, Conrad did much of his best work during my tenure. He wished at one time to be remembered mostly for *Blue Voyage, Ushant,* and the short stories "Silent Snow, Secret Snow," and "Mr. Arcularis." That is my only bid for immortality, nebulous though it be. [14]

Writing in her early eighties, Lorenz could see that her perilous relationship with Aiken was in fact part of a necessary voyage toward enlarged consciousness for both of them. Mary Hoover, the third Lorelei who immediately succeeded Lorelei Two, seemed to offer few of the necessary perils Aiken seemingly had to experience with both Lorenz and his first wife Jessie in order to move into his major phase of creativity. Lorenz had been warned before the marriage of Aiken's heavy drinking, his suicidal impulses, his cruelty; and shortly after his breakup with Jessie she was assured by mutual friends that Aiken was an emotional wreck who would soon sink forever. When Clarissa left, many predicted Aiken's collapse. One year after their separation from Clarissa, however, Aiken was once again installed in Rye, in Jeake's House, where had occurred the domestic scenes of his first two marriages. His friendship with Eliot was on the mend, and he was engaging in one of his favorite activities: drawing to him literary and intellectual notables, this time, in particular, so that Mary Hoover could paint some of them. Thus he writes Henry Murray from Rye in November, 1937:

> Tom Eliot came for the weekend, last week, played pingpong, went to church, drank his beer like a man, was in fact very good company, and promised to come down again to sit for Mary--was much impressed. And it looks as if we'd be able to get Julian Huxley and one or two other celebrities through May Sarton. Which is all to the good--I've taken the liberty of asking H.D.--Mrs. Richard Aldington (she's divorcing him)--to

---

[14]Clarissa M. Lorenz, *Lorelei Two* (Athens: The University of Georgia Press, 1983), 221-223.

look you up--she will be staying with papa Sachs sometime during the next two or three months. A fascinating by-product of psychoanalysis, if not indeed one of its disasters--do have a look at her.[15]

I quote at length to demonstrate Aiken's sociability because Lorenz uses many pages to show how withdrawn, sullen, and morose Aiken could sometimes be. Aiken was, in fact, the son of a mother who was one of Savannah's foremost socialites in the 1890s, and he never lost an inherited charm that seemed to flower after his third marriage. When the Aikens were forced by the war to move to the inherited home in Brewster, Massachusetts, called Forty-One Doors, his happiness was magnified. Thus he writes Edward Burra: "...Life here I may say is damned good--we enjoy every minute of it."[16] In Mary Hoover, Aiken had found the ideal mate for the third phase of his career, that of the growing wisdom of the man of letters. The letters reveal the erotic and creative sides of the marriage, but also the observations of those who saw the two together, including my own, have been that their relationship was based on a mutual respect and deep friendship that marriages, to be fruitful, must have. In *Ushant* Aiken calls *caritas* the love of loves. His third marriage was based, in part at least, on a large amount of both *caritas* and *philia,* the love between friends.

One may well wonder if Mary Hoover deserves to be called a Lorelei. The answer for Aiken, I believe, would be that the dangerous love of women takes more forms than erotic love. Marital contentment itself can be a form of bewitchment that draws the artist and philosopher away from his work, that urges him to give up his quest for that expanded consciousness necessary for artistic creativity. As an artist herself Mary Hoover was a companion on the quest, yet the woman's need to build and maintain a nest, D. H. Lawrence believed, could chain the male's creative instincts. It is too early to assess the personal side of Aiken's third phase, but there is no doubt that the poet believed there was an element in femininity itself that like the mother (and Aiken's mother in particular), binds the child to herself, seeks to draw the beloved male into her womb. This was doubtless what Aiken felt in his first marriage, in many ways a very successful union. Jessie McDonald, whom Aiken married in 1912, was intellectually gifted, a good mother, and an understanding wife. Aiken did not leave her to marry Clarissa Lorenz but rather, when she saw how deeply Aiken had become involved

---

[15]*Selected Letters of Conrad Aiken*, 220.
[16]Ibid., 248.

with Lorenz, she left Aiken to marry the poet's friend Martin Armstrong. Aiken was devastated by this action because of the loss of a family he greatly prized. Yet there is much evidence that Aiken's love affairs were not enough to free him from the domesticity that he loved very much but that kept him from that necessary painful step he needed to take to enter his major artistic phase.

Possibly the full involvement of marriage with Clarissa, the most perilous lover of all, was necessary for him to take the step leading to his best work. Aiken would continue all his life to maintain close relationships with his three children, and, like most dedicated artists, would use anything and everything, including his children, as subjects for his work. At the end of *Ushant*, he would use one of his daughters' visions to make his Wordsworthian point that the child is father to the man. For Aiken a few women and children intensely known were necessary for expanded consciousness even when they could also lure the artist from his life's quest. His own father, as Lorenz shows, had unconsciously taught Aiken that women lured men to their death, but Aiken through his poetical and philosophical exorcising of this paternal demon, along with many other demons, could by 1940 begin to know with his third Lorelei a kind of peace and harmony he never experienced with his other two wives. And by then he could forgive both himself and the first two Lorelei, realizing no one partner is ever fully to blame for marital disaster. *Ushant* records the calm after the storm of marital suffering, many details of which we would not have known about except for Lorenz's *Lorelei Two*. Aiken himself had described many of the problems of his first marriage in *Great Circle,* but the pain with Lorenz was doubtless too great to describe in fictional terms. Yet the end of this and the other marriage, as we see in *Ushant*, was the establishing of comradely relations even with the most difficult of partners. *Philia,* brotherly love, was to be found both during and after all three marriages, as *Ushant* makes clear.

Aiken in *Ushant* thus sums up the role of both male and female comrades in the journey of the poet. More than possibly any poet of the century who also was a critic, Aiken saw that poetry finally is not the product of the powerful ego as so many Romantics and even modernists thought it was. Poetry, Aiken believed, grew out of the communal association of many types of people. The aim of poetry, Aiken wrote Fletcher, was "advancing the consciousness and conscience and genius of mankind." The poet, he went on, is "forerunner, firebringer, orderer and releaser."[17] But, as the letters and *Ushant* show, the poet as the firebringer had to rely on a human context. Just what the nature of that poetry brought forth by the firebringer was established in large part by one of the most fruitful literary friendships in modern times: the Eliot-Aiken friendship. It is now time to consider exactly what that friendship brought forth in terms of both practical and theoretical criticism.

---

[17]Ibid., 195.

Chapter 4

Aiken and Eliot:
Poetry's Nature and Function

In his work Walt Whitman announced a kind of poetry that he believed would record a higher development in human consciousness by calling for a new kind of love that would deny all differences of gender, class, and nationality. In doing so, he challenged a painful individualistic isolation, often hidden, in the work of that Concord individualist who had inspired him, Ralph Waldo Emerson. Poe, Melville, and Hawthorne had written plainly for all to read about the agonies of modern isolation; but Whitman, having experienced this isolation also, spoke not of the overwhelming of the mind by isolation but rather of the possibility of overcoming through comradeship a growing egocentricity within the continuing movement of Romanticism. Whitman held firmly to the sacramental view of nature he had inherited from earlier Romantics like Emerson, but he put more emphasis on an intense comradeship than any American Romantic before him because he believed nature alone could not sustain the individual in his search for personal development. What was needed, Whitman taught in his best poetry, was the essential union of man, nature, and divine love, which only the great poet's vision could properly restore to a world dominated by materialism. Conrad Aiken began his own poetic career with views similar to Whitman's. Yet in other ways Aiken's poetry was so different that he would never acknowledge Whitman as a mentor.

In his first volume of poetry, *Earth Triumphant,* which he later refused to admit to his canon, Aiken proposed an optimistic, Whitmanesque viewpoint, one based on both comradeship and nature. But Aiken's concept of nature, however, was based on the philosophical naturalism being espoused by many scientists and philosophers early in the century, instead of on Whitman's transcendental vision of nature. Aiken himself was widely read in several of the natural sciences, and all of his life was aware of the complexities of modern science. His friend T. S. Eliot read the poem "Youth," from *Earth Triumphant,* in the galleys and immediately pounced on it. It was to be the first fully recorded evidence of Eliot practicing his art of criticism on Aiken. It is also evidence of a comradeship that was one of the most significant in modern literature, one that never reached the soaring heights of friendship Whitman called for but nevertheless one that proved fruitful for more than fifty years.

In an essay written at the end of his life called "A Brief Memoir of Harvard, Dean Briggs and T. S. Eliot," Aiken tells us of his poem "Youth," of which Eliot remarked "that the hero was perhaps not as innocent and romantic as he was made out to be, and maybe carried rubber goods in his hip pocket." Aiken continues: "And of the book at large, that it was 'wrinkled with thought.' How true. Of *Turns and Movies*, 1916, he observed in a letter, 'anything which can so disgust, must have power.'"[1] Eliot in his discernment of meaning and in his evaluation of Aiken's first book-length poem plunges right to the heart of Aiken's continuing poetic problem, and Aiken more than fifty years later admitted it. Aiken's second book-length work, *Turns and Movies*, Eliot says, has imaginative power, but he also notes a painful disgust arising from his reading of the book. Aiken had moved already by 1916 from posing as a Romantic innocent, partly in the Whitman vein, to dealing with what would be his chief subject for much of his literary career, the painful condition of his own inner life. Thus Aiken moved from an idealistic youthful Romanticism to the kind of painful modern idiom associated first with Baudelaire, and, later, more with Eliot than with any English-speaking poet in this century. Aiken was glad to have Eliot reading over his shoulder, making sometimes painful comments. Later in life Aiken as critic would make even more painful comments about Eliot's work. Both poets, in spite of the pain they inflicted on each other and the distrust they sometimes felt for each other, would never cease being friends.

Eliot and Aiken were at Harvard more than literary comrades coediting the *Advocate*. In his brief memoir Aiken says simply that Eliot "was an older brother, and sometimes a stern one."[2] Aiken did not use the term brother lightly. He had grown up in a tightly knit family with two younger brothers and a younger sister. As the oldest child, he had been at the very center of his mother and father's attention, and before he was ten had seen his father become an ogre who beat him regularly for nothing and a mother whose consciousness was worn ragged by growing fears of violence and death. After the murder-suicide of his parents Aiken would choose to go alone to New England while his brothers went to Philadelphia and were adopted by

---

[1] *The Clerk's Journal: Being the Diary of a Queer Man*: (New York The Eakins Press, 1971), 6.

[2] Ibid.

Frederick Windslow Taylor, the inventor of the time-and-motion study. Aiken would never be close to his siblings after 1901, and thus his calling Eliot a brother has great poignancy if one understands the poet's belief in and continuing need for family life.

In my own conversations with Aiken in the 1960s, I believe that the most emotion he ever showed in discussing anyone was when Eliot's name came up from time to time. He had, by the time of his Harvard years, as *Ushant* shows, rediscovered a sense of family with his mother's relatives in New England, and his charm and love of people, as his letters clearly indicate, would give him a wide circle of friends and acquaintances. Yet there is a personal depth in the Aiken-Eliot relationship not found anywhere in Aiken's life except in his early family life in Savannah and in his relationships with his three wives; in fact, Aiken's wives all made an impact on the relationship with Eliot because Aiken's restlessness with his own growing domesticity with Jessie and their children in the early twenties is paralleled by a growing rift that appeared in the Aiken-Eliot friendship, possibly because of the growth of Eliot's role as Anglo-American literary arbiter, beginning with his editorship of *The Criterion* in 1922.

During the years of Lorelei Two the relationship seemed to sour. Clarissa Lorenz goes into the Eliot-Aiken relationship only once, and then she quotes Margaret Nash on the subject of Eliot ignoring Aiken's work during the late twenties and the thirties, which was the period of the poet's greatest creativity:

> Margaret told me that T. S. Eliot, then editor of the *Criterion*, ordered a copy of *Great Circle* after hearing that it was magnificent, then delivered a double entendre to Paul: 'Each book Aiken writes is better than the last one.' When Margaret chided the editor of *New Verse* for rejecting Conrad's poems, he said he had taken Eliot's word that they were unsuitable. She suspected Eliot of being at the bottom of the resistance movement. Regarding his old friend as subversive, a rival who must remain crushed, he staged a cabal, feeling it his duty as a Catholic to stamp out atheism and nihilism.[3]

This is a damning indictment and one that Lorenz does not question in her book. Eliot's religious bigotry is well known, but it must also be remembered

---

[3]Clarissa M. Lorenz, *Lorelei Two* (Athens: The University of Georgia Press, 1983), 172.

that during the period between 1926 and 1936 the two men were both caught up in painful relationships with women, Eliot with his first wife Vivien and Aiken with Clarissa. In the early thirties both were sometimes uncertain about their creative gifts as they began to write what many consider to be their major works, Eliot the *Quartets* and Aiken the Preludes and *Ushant*. Above all, however, it is Aiken we must turn to concerning the meaning of this difficult yet very fruitful literary comradeship.

I have already suggested how Aiken, with the help of his third wife Mary, began to renew his relationship with Eliot. Aiken told me that he saw less and less of Eliot when his friend increasingly associated in the early twenties with Lady Rothermere and others who would help him launch *The Criterion.* As editor of *The Criterion,* Eliot would become a literary arbiter and with his critical essays would establish himself as the most influential literary critic writing in English in this century. Yet a new closeness with Eliot would increasingly emerge as Aiken himself finally experienced with Mary a fruitful and lasting marital relationship. After Eliot married Valerie in 1957, the relationship between the two couples became extremely warm. Valerie was particularly close to Aiken and visited him in America after Eliot's death. Aiken's own assessment of his relationship with Eliot was that the affection had never abated between the two men but that there had been a painful separation during much of the twenties and thirties. Looking back in *Ushant* on the meaning of this separation beginning in the early twenties, Aiken reveals a characteristic charity:

> [H]e [Eliot] had built the splendid ramparts round that rare new domain of his, and behind them he had become all but invisible, all but intangible: the affection between them was not to have been diminished but the distance between them was sensible and would increase. But was it so certain that this was in any degree a misfortune, or that it might not have occurred anyway (*Ushant*, 215).

Long before Hugh Kenner had seen Eliot's invisibility as a key factor in his life and work, Aiken had observed Eliot's strong desire to hide himself behind self-erected ramparts. Aiken's charity, of course, is ironic because Eliot, moving into Anglo-Catholicism, was deserting for a time his oldest and best literary friend whereas Aiken, a known renegade from established religion though not an atheist as Lorenz believed him to be, was showing at the time of Eliot's separation more charity and generosity than even in his younger years when he forgot for a time his own work to become an advocate with Pound of Eliot's poems. Yet Aiken's charity was typical of much of his life. He has suffered because of his parents and his two brothers, but he would forgive them all even as he forgave Eliot and Clarissa Lorenz.

Aiken thus learned to accept himself and others in a way that would make a new closeness both to Eliot and to a new wife possible. After all, part of his pilgrimage toward greater consciousness consisted in freeing himself from entanglements created by bitterness and the psychic trauma that often occurs in close relationships between writers. Aiken in the thirties had begun to understand what Joyce had been writing about in *Ulysses* and what he in a similar but lesser novel, *Blue Voyage*, had also written about: humans must relate to each other to be truly human but that all relationships inevitably are love-hate relationships. The best one could do was to minimize the destructive aspect as much as possible. One way that Aiken chose to do this was to accept Eliot's poetry and his pilgrimage as valid even though different from his own. Thus Aiken assessed the journey of his friend into Anglicanism:

> [M]ounting from cataract to cataract, or hierarchy to hierarchy, of accepted order, he would at last achieve what no American ichthyolater had achieved before him, and find himself, at Canterbury, after the pilgrimage of pilgrimages, in the very presence of the Ichthos itself. That the achievement was unique and astounding and attended, too, by rainbows of creative splendor, there could be no doubt. Indeed, it was in the nature of a miracle, a transformation. But was it not to have been, also a surrender, and perhaps the saddest known to D. in his life (*Ushant*, 216)?

For all the pain Aiken suffered because of Eliot, he never gave up on their friendship between the two or on the greatness of Eliot's poetry, which for him exceeded that of any modern poetry in English. Yet he could not accept Eliot's conversion to Anglicanism because he believed it to be a step into the past. But Aiken did not follow those many critics who from the time of Eliot's conversion in 1927 to the present have continued to insist that Eliot ceased to be a great poet when he became Anglo-Catholic. Aiken looked carefully, as the good critic should, at the later poetry and made his own evaluation of that poetry. For Aiken, Eliot's *Quartets* represented real poetic accomplishment, and Eliot at the end of his life would be for Aiken the man whose name should characterize the modern age. Thus Aiken, in a *Life* magazine article that he was asked to write a few day's after Eliot's death, would say: "In any case, our age beyond any doubt has been, and will continue to be, the Age of Eliot."[4] Aiken believed this because for him Eliot had always had great poetic gifts, had developed his gifts in a way his friend Lowry had not developed his, and, finally, had addressed himself to writing some of the greatest visionary poetry of the century.

The purpose of poetry, then, is at the center of the critic's task-- that kind of critic who, like Aiken, Pound or Eliot himself, is also a teacher concerned with the most significant poetry that can be written in a given age. All three accepted gladly, even at the risk of sometimes falling into arrogance and error, criticism's chief task of evaluating literary works. Beyond this they believed they could also define the nature of poetry in their own age, while at the same time attempting to write this kind of poetry. Everything in the best and most influential criticism of all three springs from this task of evaluation that they first accepted as young men.

Thus Eliot evaluated Aiken's early work even as Aiken early saw in "Prufrock" one of the important modern poems and urged Pound to take the same view, which he immediately did. Aiken believed that the critic should examine the psychological roots of the modern poet's pilgrimage, which at its best was a search for expanded consciousness. In writing of Eliot's "pilgrimage of pilgrimages" in *Ushant*, Aiken revealed that Eliot's view was the same. For Aiken the great poets since Goethe were essentially pilgrims seeking light and understanding, and inevitably their works at their best recorded this pilgrimage. Aiken made a concern for pilgrimage central to his criticism whereas Eliot's criticism ignores the psychological aspects of the quest. Nevertheless, the best work of both poets often reveals a similar quest for expanded consciousness and love. Aiken in *Ushant* explains his own "persistent effort to find for himself a literary *modus vivendi* which would keep that consistent view of his at its constant center" (*Ushant*, 246).

Then he goes on to say that there was "even more to it than that. Consciousness, yes--one was automatically enough implicated in that, from the outset." That thing beyond the central concern for consciousness was then defined in this way: "for if it was the writer's business, or the poet's, to be as conscious as possible, and his primary obligation, then wouldn't this impose upon him the still deeper obligation of being conscious of his *own* workings, the workings of his psyche." (*Ushant*, 246). Aiken records how he discusses the problem with John Gould Fletcher and with Eliot and even

---

[4]Conrad Aiken, "T. S. Eliot," *Life*, January 15, 1965, 93.

persuades Eliot to accept his essay written on this subject for the *Criterion*. Eliot, "with competent irony" essentially rejected Aiken's offering of a work that included what Aiken called the crystal and the matrix, the background of the work itself. Fundamentally, T. S. Eliot could not accept the view of the poet offered by Aiken because he was in the twenties working at the very center of the modern tradition of symbolism, and Aiken was still seeking to mediate between an older Romanticism and the new modernist poetry. The poet through symbolism sought invisibility, but Aiken never gave up the confessional aspect of Romanticism. Furthermore, Aiken was moving in the direction, without ever really knowing it, of surrealism.

Aiken's search for an acceptable role for the poet is a part of his continuing efforts to understand the nature and function of poetry. Eliot erected ramparts around his new poetic domain by imitating those symbolists who hid themselves in their poetry and in various ivory towers to escape a world they feared. For Balakian, the typical French symbolist is one who writes complex poetry and who withdraws from ordinary life, becoming finally obsessed with decay and death. This withdrawal helps to explain the pessimism of the symbolists. But Yeats, who early was drawn personally to Mallarmé and his Parisian circle, decided on a different course. He went into the world seeking not death but life, yet he also hid himself behind a series of masks. For Yeats the mask was necessary to protect the poet, and Eliot was doubtless imitating Yeats in arranging his own set of masks in order to make himself invisible. As Eliot became more important in the literary world his personality in fact did almost become invisible. Aiken, while barely holding his own in the literary world, became more than ever the poet seeking a role in a world that had little place for one who clung to many Romantic viewpoints. Aiken increasingly saw himself as the kind of poet who spends his whole life developing his poetic consciousness while at the same time expressing his personal viewpoint in his own poetry, fiction, and criticism. Reuel Denney in his perceptive study of Aiken notes that an anonymous writer in the *Times Literary Supplement* of 19 April 1963 put his finger on Aiken's personal devotion to the art of poetry by saying that "increasingly poetry has become a way of writing not a way of thinking" and then suggests that Aiken, like Shelley, is capable of "thinking in poetic terms; that is to say with the whole consciousness."[5] Nothing written about Aiken's essential genius has put it better, this idea of attempting to devote the

---

[5]Reuel Denney, *Conrad Aiken* (Minneapolis: University of Minnesota Press, 1964), 44-45.

whole consciousness to poetry. This accomplishment, together with what the same reviewer calls a "cosmic sense that outsoars Eliot and Pound," links Aiken to the movement, chiefly French, called surrealism.[6] It also helps to distinguish Aiken as a critic from a movement that Eliot above all others helped to launch that came to be called the New Criticism.

Aiken himself was in many ways part of the New Criticism. When I. A. Richards discovered that his Cambridge students could write little that was meaningful about poems he passed out to them, he sought in his book *Practical Criticism* to bring to literary criticism an awareness of meaning in individual works. He was combating an impressionistic criticism that grew out of a decadent late Romanticism, itself a revolt against the moralistic criticism of the Victorians. The study of literature had become for some educators a recounting of the biographies of poets, and for others it was an exploration of moral "messages." For some, literature afforded the opportunity for vague, impressionistic statements that said little that was meaningful about the work itself. It was time, Richards believed, to return to the individual work itself and to its various meanings. Richards is well known for the study of meaning, but it should not be forgotten that he also could and did evaluate works of the new modern poetry. By 1920 he understood the importance of Eliot's poetry; and soon after that he recognized the value of Aiken's criticism. Aiken finally met Richards on his Spanish vacation with Lowry in 1931, and an immediate rapport was established.

Eliot, Aiken, and Richards as critics were all three devoted to the work itself. They fully realized how much had been lost because of too much attention paid to authors, to their philosophies, and to their intentions. Also they believed the work should be evaluated on its own merit, and they were not afraid of such evaluations, many of which would have important consequences for literary history in this century. Eliot's evaluations are too well known to need discussion, but the lesser known criticism of Aiken in the 1920s and afterward made important evaluative contributions that would influence the reputations of figures as diverse as Emily Dickinson, Herman Melville, and William Faulkner. Arthur Waterman in describing Aiken's critical achievement points to the poet's remarkable success in the most difficult of critical tasks, that of evaluation: "Since he did not evade his responsibility to judge the work before him and since in writing reviews he had to judge quickly, without any guidance but that of his good taste, we

---

[6]Ibid., 44.

would expect that many of his first guesses do not hold up."[7] Waterman points out that Aiken did indeed reverse himself on Lawrence and qualify his response to Eliot but concludes that "again and again one is struck by how *right* Aiken usually was, how accurate and how pertinent were his initial assessments." And thus Waterman concludes his assessment of Aiken's evaluative criticism: "His record of 'firsts' is probably unequaled by any other modern critic."[8] Aiken himself, looking back over forty years of writing reviews would conclude concerning his evaluative efforts: some of his immaturity as a young critic is "partly redeemed . . . by what I quite enviously confess to have been an uncanny sort of foresightedness."[9] Aiken then concludes in his Preface to *A Reviewer's ABC* that he was writing his criticism primarily in an effort to state "where he *wanted* to go and where also he wanted poetry, fiction, and criticism to go."[10]

Aiken's chief literary motive in writing criticism was to help shape the emerging new modernist tradition. Thus he was, along with critics like Eliot, Pound, Richards, and Leavis, bringing to birth the New Criticism through a close scrutiny of individual works. But Aiken could never follow the paths the New Criticism would take as it became after World War II the established form of criticism in universities. Adherents of a strict formalism, like Cleanth Brooks, whose perceptive criticism often tended to judge poetry primarily by the categories of wit, paradox, and irony, created an academic formalism that sometimes seemed to be cut off from the early New Critical concern for myth, ritual, and symbol. Even John Crowe Ransom, whose book, *The New Criticism* established the name of the movement, found that his concern for structure and texture was not enough, that myth as the basis of poetry should be placed at the center of criticism. Inevitably formalism would lose its appeal as structuralism in the 1960s and deconstruction in the seventies and eighties would erect new theories concerning the nature of poetry.

Theory in fact would by the eighties dominate criticism. Aiken, almost from the beginning of his work as publishing critic, would be armed with theories to explain the reason for his judgments, which, as Waterman seems

---

[7]Arthur Waterman, "Conrad Aiken as Critic: The Consistent View," *Mississippi Quarterly* 24 (Spring, 1971), 107.

[8]Ibid.

[9]Ibid., 107

[10]Rufus Blanchard, *Collected Criticism of Conrad Aiken from 1916 to the Present: A Reviewer's ABC* (New York: Meridian Books, 1958).

to say, were not based on guesswork. Richards in 1919 had seen in Aiken's *Scepticisms* an important theory, one that poetry was a natural product with discoverable functions open to analysis. But analysis alone, Aiken realized, could not take the place of evaluation, which inevitably had to spring from a metaphysical viewpoint. Rufus Blanchard in his introduction to *A Reviewer's ABC* sums up Aiken's most important critical theory concerning the nature of poetry:

> And since the value of the work depends on the effect it has on the similarly complex mechanism of the observer, there is no absolute scheme of values by which the critic can judge it. . . . It follows that criticism must deal also, then, with the function of art--with its psycho- and socio-therapeutic uses.[11]

Aiken's theory is as old as Aristotle's evaluation of Greek tragedy in terms of the concept of purification, or purgation, of the audience, of catharsis, that is. It is found in modern criticism in Kenneth Burke's concept of art as a form of medicine or Norman Holland's study of reader responses. Art, for Aiken, served the psychological needs of individuals; it was effective to the extent that it had the capacity, as Waterman puts it, to "heal the pain of living."[12] Yet this theory must also be placed alongside the most basic quest of the individual, which for Aiken was the search for expanded consciousness. Vision, or expanded consciousness, is what the individual seeks most deeply in his involvement with art, Aiken tells us, and it is vision that separates true art from those forms of pseudo-art that only provide a drug for psychic pain. Expanded consciousness brings with it psychic growth and love, Freud believed, as did Jung and Rank, Aiken tells us.

Where Aiken most differed from Eliot in his criticism was in his concern for both the creative process and for the pilgrimage that would allow the artist to encounter the mysterious powers that made creativity possible. As Waterman puts it, Aiken, as a Romantic, believed that "no one, not even the artist, can fully account for what happens in the moment of creativity, because that moment occurs in the unconscious." Eliot's criticism ignores the role of the unconscious in criticism and what Aiken called the "magic" in art. Thus Waterman continues:

---

[11]Ibid., 49.
[12]Waterman, 97.

Creation is 'magic,' something that defies analysis and cannot be caused or measured. Once 'inspiration' has happened, however, the intelligence and craft of the artist take over to shape that impulse into a finished work.[13]

Aiken's use of terms out of the Romantic tradition helps at times to make his criticism seem old fashioned, yet it was his encounter with his own unconscious mind, as well as his intelligent observation of his own and other people's response to literature, that made it possible for him to recognize the literary value for modern readers of figures as diverse as Melville, Dickinson, Stevens, Eliot, Thomas, Lorca, Lowry, Lawrence, and Joyce. Where Aiken is more modern in his approach to criticism than Eliot is in his emphasis on exact and dispassionate analysis. By comparison, Eliot's criticism, for all its influence--due primarily to certain incisive comments that seized the modern critical mind--seems authoritarian in the manner of a schoolmaster prepared to rap the knuckles of all readers not conversant with Eliot's personal version of the "great tradition." In the place of authoritarianism Aiken substitutes careful analysis and consistency of viewpoint. At his best he is as carefully analytical as those university critics who installed the New Criticism in the academies of the West. Of this aspect of his role as critic, Jay Martin tells us, that Aiken in his criticism sought to put his primary emphasis on an analysis and discernment that were as exact as possible.[14] Exactness is one of the key concepts in Aiken's criticism, and it reflects that side of Aiken that accepted fully the role of modern science and the role of a university like his beloved Harvard in preserving a record as well as extending an understanding of the creative works of humankind.

Yet even as the reader explores Aiken's struggle to understand and explain the literature of the past and the present, he continually confronts a quality that seems old-fashioned in the modern age, something strangely Romantic. It repels many readers, even as it often repelled Eliot. It is the quality of personalism, the concept to which Whitman clung, that maintains that the best creative efforts constitute a shared activity. The concept is mainly found in a later Romantic like Whitman or even Lawrence rather than in the first Romantics, who, though exalting love, often were caught up in their own poetic egos. We see it is the modern philosopher Gabriel Marcel

---

[13]Ibid.

[14]Jay Martin, *Conrad Aiken: A Life of His Art* (Princeton: Princeton University Press, 1962), 98.

and in one of his followers, Walker Percy. Marcel, and Percy with him, took up the idea of Sören Kierkegaard that a full awareness of subjectivity, or the personal element in existence, was necessary for a life to be authentic, or fully human. But Marcel went beyond subjectivity to the concept of intersubjectivity. To be too much concerned with one's own subjectivity was not enough. Authentic existence requires a relationship with the subjective aspects of others, a relationship that Marcel called intersubjectivity. Percy and Aiken, without ever having encountered each other's work, are remarkably similar in their belief that the world can and should be approached both objectively and subjectively. For them both approaches are necessary if the individual is to understand and be able to evaluate both the sciences and the arts.[15] Aiken's literary criticism, therefore, represents an attempt to analyze works of literature from both subjective and objective viewpoints. At the same time Aiken believed that inevitably the artist fully engaged in the literary life must relate both subjectively and objectively to certain other artists. Intersubjectivity for Aiken was, however, not always a creative event; often it involved great risks.

The Aiken-Eliot relationship cannot be understood without taking into account the risks both poets took in their involvement with each other. Eliot in his last play, *The Elder Statesman*, sums up in his character Gomez various ambivalent feelings he had toward Aiken. Gomez doubtless contains elements of several writers close to Eliot, but much in the relationship between the protagonist of the play, a prominent figure in his chosen field, and a somewhat disrespectable man fallen on bad days resembles the Eliot-Aiken relationship between 1922 and 1937. The two men in the play seem strikingly different from each other, yet the protagonist is forced at last to acknowledge an underlying connection with his former friend. In his *Paris Review* interview Eliot tries to distance himself from Aiken's poems: "We were friends but I don't think we influenced each other at all" and, referring to his own poems that Aiken first showed to Pound in 1914, Eliot writes, "He thought Pound might like them, though they were very different from his." Interestingly enough, in the light of the character Gomez and his Latin associations, Eliot says of Aiken: "When it came to foreign writers, he was

---

[15]My comparative study of Aiken and Walker Percy, *The Writer as Shaman: The Pilgrimages of Conrad Aiken and Walker Percy* (Macon: Mercer University Press, 1986), traces the many similarities between the two writers and shows how both writers sought to balance an objective view of the universe with a subjective view. Thus they sought to reveal connections between science and literature.

more interested in Italian and Spanish, and I was all for the French."[16] Yet part of the pain Aiken suffered as a result of his close relationship with Eliot resulted from the continuing refusal of Eliot and even many Eliot scholars to admit that Aiken did have a real poetic influence on his friend.

Finally in 1979 Fred D. Crawford revealed the full extent of Eliot's debt to Aiken in *The Waste Land*. Joseph Warren Beach and others had seemingly established the dictum that, as Crawford puts it, "Aiken's influence on Eliot was negligible or coincidental." Crawford, however, not only records that "throughout *The Waste Land*, Eliot echoed and parodied Aiken's 'The Divine Pilgrim' to such an extent that Aiken immediately recognized it," he also records Aiken's generous comment to Robert Linscott that "the borrowing made no difference to one essential fact: 'it's the best thing I've seen in years.'"[17] Aiken's loyalty both to his friend and his awareness of his own role as a critic who is objective, subjective, and intersubjective kept him from bitterness. Yet in *Ushant* he would record the pain he inevitably experienced in his relationship with Eliot during much of the period of the twenties and thirties.

Crawford concludes his study of the influence of Aiken on Eliot with lines from Aiken's parody of *The Waste Land* written in a letter to Linscott. The parody begins "Eliot is the cruellest poet, breeding/ lyrics under the driest dustpan ."[18] Aiken's continuing awareness of the cruel streak in Eliot's nature is summed up in the name he bestows on Eliot in *Ushant*: Tsetse.

Like his appellation for Pound, Rabbi Ben Ezra, its significance cannot be appreciated unless one is aware of the deepest feeling Aiken had for the two poets. For Pound, Aiken felt respect and admiration for the superb gifts this literary pioneer had as teacher and artistic guide. But Pound, wanting primarily to be a great modern poet, hated his own best qualities, which most resembled those of a great rabbi. The result was possibly a kind of Freudian projection of self-hatred, because of rejection and isolation, onto the Jews, the most international and artistically cognizant of all ethnic groups of the early twentieth century, from whom sprang great interpreters of the modern arts, individuals in many ways much like Pound himself. Hidden

---

[16]"T. S. Eliot," *Writers at Work: The Paris Review Interviews, Second Series*, ed. George Plimpton (New York: The Viking Press, 1963), 94, 95.

[17]Fred D. Crawford, "Conrad Aiken's Canceled Debt to T. S. Eliot," *Journal of Modern Literature* VII, 3 (September 1974), 416, *432*.

[18]Ibid, 432.

self-hatred in Pound brought forth a fanaticism and prejudice that eventually separated him from the politically liberal Aiken, who sometimes made international Jews significant figures in his work. But Aiken could never be separated from Eliot, himself sometimes anti-Semitic, because he knew that this man was always until death his older brother. Still the most dangerous aspect of that brother, an aspect hidden from Eliot himself, had to be faced continually if there was to be lasting comradeship. The flaw, summed up by the metaphor of the African fly that causes sleeping sickness, was Eliot's pride and will to literary mastery over others. After all, Eliot had proclaimed his periodical to be not a literary criterion but *the* criterion. The effect of this pride on Aiken, the younger brother, was the projection of a psychic sleeping sickness that sometimes denied the existence of both the younger poet and his works.

Thus the "cruellest poet," as Aiken called him, could claim at will the work of his friend and then deny the existence of that friend's work. The cruelty could even become sadistic, and yet Aiken could place that sadism in the context of Eliot's larger kindness: thus in *Ushant* Aiken would write that "it was that evident streak of sadism in the Tsetse's otherwise urbane and kindly character, which now and again, as D. well knew, he enjoyed indulging (*Ushant*)." What made a continuing comradeship possible was Aiken's forgiveness of his friend. I have elsewhere established the fact of the continuing fruitfulness of the Aiken-Eliot relationship, basing my conclusions on several discussions with Aiken himself and on candid remarks in *Ushant*.[19]

What made it possible was the continuing ability of both to accept the faults of each other, but deeper than this ability to forgive was the similarity of their poetic paths, a fact I will continue to allude to in my discussion of Aiken's poetic pilgrimage. In their growing awareness of the nature and function of poetry, beginning with their efforts to analyze and evaluate dispassionately the works of many different writers, they discovered continually what Aiken described as the function of poetry, that is, the best way human beings have of expressing anything. They were not afraid of risking themselves poetically on many levels. They collaborated on pornographic poetry, the *King Bolo* poems, as students at Harvard, where both began their literary careers; they tried their hand successfully at light verse--Eliot with his *Practical Cats* and Aiken with limericks--and they both

---

[19]See my article, "Conrad Aiken and T. S. Eliot" in *Essays in Arts and Sciences,* 7, no. 1 (May 1978).

helped to create in English a kind of wasteland poetry not before seen. In mid-career they began to discover the meaning of psychic growth through some of the most important deliberative and philosophical poetry of the century. They are most alike in rediscovering the various "natures" of poetry in our time without ever establishing an extended theory concerning the nature of poetry. Unlike Wordsworth and Coleridge--a more famous pair of literary comrades--they never allowed their friendship to dissolve because, for at least one reason, each had something important both personally and artistically to contribute to the other.

Explorations like that of Fred D. Crawford will continue to reveal ways in which the lesser poet, Aiken, led the greater poet Eliot. Eliot's immersion in French symbolism did not in itself provide the full impetus for Eliot's writing of *The Waste Land*. James E. Miller, Jr., in *T. S. Eliot's Personal Waste Land*, has studied the many personal aspects of the poem in order to reveal Eliot's need to exorcize certain personal demons in his unconscious mind. At least part of Eliot's impetus to face his own personal wasteland, as Crawford demonstrates, came from reading Aiken's own wasteland poems, which themselves reveal Aiken's attempt to exorcize the demons, many of them sexual, within his own unconscious mind. To understand what Aiken was doing one needs the insights of Jacques Derrida and the deconstructionist critics. Derrida, Jonathan Culler tells us, calls "the rationality which treats meanings as concepts or logical representations that it is the function of signs to express" the "'logocentrism' of Western culture."[20] Culler goes on to say that "One deconstructs this perspective by arguing that the differences ultimately responsible for meaning did not fall from heaven but are themselves products."[21] For Aiken, Derrida's *difference*, that necessary building block of deconstruction, was the individual products of each unconscious mind. Culler, like many who see deconstruction as only an aspect of a semiotics that can never be really deconstructed because the "source of meanings is no longer a consciousness in which they exist prior to their expression," denies what was fundamental to Aiken and possibly to Derrida, which is that real deconstruction is a necessary aspect of any true literary movement because the act of decomposition, a word Derrida has used to define deconstruction, is necessary to exorcize certain logocentric

---

[20]Jonathan Culler, *The Pursuit of Signs: Semiotics, Literature, Deconstruction* (Ithaca, N.Y.: Cornell University Press, 1981), 40.
[21]Ibid.

gods enshrined in the unconscious.[22]   Before a creative expansion of consciousness can occur there must be that affirmative *yes* Derrida celebrates in Joyce's *Ullyses*; with his own *yes* Aiken decomposes many logocentric idols of his moralistic upbringing.

A deconstructive viewpoint is also valuable in understanding the role of intertextuality in the criticism of Aiken and Eliot. The latter's use of the concept of "tradition" in criticism is well known, but Aiken's intertextual viewpoint, which is far more comprehensive than Eliot's, is less well understood. Of his approach to texts in his criticism, Waterman has written:

> In lieu of Pound's penchant for novelty, Aiken prefers to compare a contemporary work or writer with an established name from the past: Katherine Mansfield with Chekhov, Virginia Woolf with Jane Austen, Eliot with Erasmus, to mention a few. By this comparative method Aiken can weigh the new against the old in order to discover how it is new, which is frequently a matter of education; and whether or not it has any value, which is chiefly a matter of taste.[23]

The word *taste* is here significant above others because for Aiken the critical process was still something mysterious, but also it was a form of discourse open to any intelligent and interested reader or writer. For that reason, Aiken has said, he chose to avoid the philosophical complexities of the kind of theoretical criticism beginning to emerge after World War I in the work of I. A. Richards. His own philosophy sprang from James and Santayana and was pragmatic and not theoretical. The result was a kind of intelligent but clearly stated criticism that was by 1940 being ignored by many.

Aiken in his criticism and in his literary life generally could never desert his personalistic viewpoint long enough to be as philosophically abstract as criticism was becoming in the hands of some New Critics. In 1941 he noticed the tendency of the New Criticism to speak increasingly in a private language, which he castigates in a letter to Cowley:

> I confess I don't see it all, the ramifications of the party-lines in the present battle of the books becomes too complex and changes too often for any careful or exact scrutiny. But fun, just the same. I think the Tate-to-Blackmur-to-Winters-to-Brooks (Cleanth)-to Ransom

---

[22]Ibid.
[23]Waterman, "Conrad Aiken as Critic: The Consistent View," 99.

roundelay is becoming a menace, and with widening rings, and ought to be dealt with, but they're tough babies. And that O-so-private language of theirs! Jesus.[24]

Yet in spite of his denigration of leading New Critics, paralleled in this period by his criticism of Eliot for being too intellectual, his comradeship with Tate and Ransom would not be dimmed. Tate would be only slightly less a friend than Eliot. Aiken believed that Tate and Ransom, among others, continued the dialogue of a public criticism necessary for the writing of literary masterpieces. As for "Brooks (Cleanth)," this archon of modern criticism thus continued into the eighties to be an important supporter of Aiken's literary achievements. As Aiken continued to praise Eliot in the years after his death in 1965, so Brooks was a continuing supporter of Aiken's reputation. Thus comradeship, growing out of personal relationships, has continued in an age of deconstruction to undergird the American literary experience.

What had begun to change, as Aiken after 1940 reiterates in his letters, is a turning away from an emphasis on feelings and unconscious aspects of the human being in favor of intelligence alone. In his letter to Cowley attacking the private language of the New Critics, he notes that he was savagely attacked in print by Randall Jarrell for an *Atlantic* article that offered his "plea for romanticism." Then he asks in the letter, concerning Jarrell's attack: ". . . but why should this add up to such a monstrous hate?"[25] By 1941 Aiken was criticizing Eliot for too much intellectualism in his poetry. What his plea for Romanticism amounted to was a calling for an emphasis on emotions that the original Romantics had celebrated--love, joy, and hope. Doubtless the utmost seriousness of World War II had caused poets to ignore the Romantic call for personal feelings. Yet it was the kind of active hate that Aiken found in Jarrell's attack that was a signal for the eclipse his work as critic and poet would, before its rediscovery, undergo for nearly twenty years.

The rediscovery of Aiken's work began in the early 1960s, itself a Romantic decade of hopes and of a renewed sense of love, wonder, and awe. The decade was also open to the kind of confessional writing that most New Critics denigrated. But by 1960 the New Criticism as a movement was collapsing. Structuralism and later deconstruction would replace it as major

---

[24] *Selected Letters of Conrad Aiken*, 252-253.
[25] Ibid., 252.

critical movements in the West, yet the personalism of the 1960s would not totally die out as the extravagances of the decade were rejected in the seventies. The interest in Eliot in particular would continue unabated and with it a smaller interest in Aiken. Changes that occurred in Eliot the man after his successful second marriage doubtless had something to do with the coming changes of the 1960s. From the time that Eliot spoke to 14,000 people in 1955 at the University of Minnesota down through the late eighties when the musical *Cats,* based on *Old Possum's Book of Practical Cats*, was being performed throughout the world, the poet has remained on the public mind. And increasingly there has been the demand to know more about Eliot the man.

Eliot's own personality revealed itself increasingly after 1957. Ackroyd tells us that in 1958 Eliot and his wife visited Texas and "asked why the young men seemed so gloomy when there was so much to be happy about." It was as if he were proclaiming an end to an overserious decade of academic criticism, thus announcing a new decade when personal happiness should accompany the quest for a tradition. On the same trip, he met Aiken in Cambridge where, Ackroyd says, "he publicly embraced his old friend, Conrad Aiken, moving Aiken almost to tears."[26] The rediscovery of their friendship would come into its own after this time. It was as if both men were announcing to the world that personal feelings do matter greatly, that they can even be displayed in public. When Aiken in his *Life* article in 1965, shortly after Eliot's death, announced that the modernist period between 1920 and 1960 would eventually be called the Age of Eliot, he was announcing in effect that the kind of poetic pilgrimage he and Eliot and other modernists had begun early in the century was in fact the central literary effort of that period. It was, he seems to say, a movement that began with symbolism but that in time brought forth a modern version of Romanticism, that is to say, a new affirmation based on both creative emotional insights as well as on intellectual and visionary insights. The *Life* article was but one of many statements by Aiken that affirmed the continuing quest of two friends for an understanding of poetry's nature and function that would make sense in a century that had challenged the primacy of poetry as a means of human expression.

---

[26]Peter Ackroyd, *T. S. Eliot: A Life* (New York: Simon and Schuster, 1984), 323.

Chapter 5

The Poet as Pilgrim

Aiken is linked to his two most important early poet-friends--John Gould Fletcher and T. S. Eliot--by a significant concern for the use of musical parallels in poetry. In her comprehensive work on the subject of music and poetry, *Musical Influence on American Poetry,* Charmenz S. Lenhart discusses the uses of music made by the three poets and clearly points to Aiken as the modern poet who "most fully developed in American verse the possibilities of musical parallels." She points out that Aiken--like Poe, Whitman, and Lanier, all of whom he occasionally resembles--owes "the nebulous quality of his imagery, which critics have sometimes deplored--to the fact that he is working always with the musical parallel in mind."[1] Critics like Calvin S. Brown and Robert Emerson Carlile have tended to approach Aiken almost exclusively from the standpoint of his musical qualities. The poet's acute awareness of music is but one aspect of his Romantic viewpoint, an awareness that links him to the Romantic sides of both Eliot and Fletcher. Yet he writes to Cowley in 1946 of his early poetic career: "Here you can see a young man who fondly thought he was seeking a kind of absolute music in word and verse, while in reality he was embarking unknown to himself, on a psychoanalytic celebration of the consciousness of modern man."[2] He goes on to call this whole process his "self-unwinding." Aiken as a critic of his own work, at least in the letters, is not always trustworthy because of the oscillation of his moods. Yet there is an awareness in the above statement of the two major aspects of his poetic genius, the former the musical and Romantic self he never altogether lost and the other a deconstructive self who accepts the chaos within his own psyche and within modern society. Yet the word "celebration" suggests the rediscovery of a lost harmony, a momentary glimpse of an aspect of a joy found amidst fragmentation.

Critics of Aiken since 1960 have generally emphasized the fragmented aspect of Aiken's pilgrimage, an aspect found in most of his best poetry and summed up in *Ushant.* What they have tended to neglect is the musical

---

[1]Charmenz S. Lenhart, *Musical Influence on Poetry* (Athens: The University of Georgia Press, 1956), 290.

[2]Joseph Killorin, *Selected Letters of Conrad Aiken* (New Haven: Yale University Press, 1978), 268.

inspiration hidden behind his literary expression of pilgrimage. As a writer who thought of himself as fully modern and as a poet working at least partly in the symbolist tradition, Aiken sees his own modern consciousness as a fragmented one shorn of the usual foundations of belief and exposed to a modern fragmenting chaos. Yet Houston Peterson in his first book-length study of Aiken emphasizes the poet's awareness of both chaos and of a melody contained within that perceived chaos, a melody that must be discovered to sustain an existence that often seems meaningless. In his greatest poems, the philosophical Preludes of the thirties, Aiken maintains his musical awareness while continuing to encounter his own inner chaos and that of the modern world. Peterson and Henry A. Murray belong to a group of critics who have perceived that Aiken seizes from chaos a truth for himself that releases his own creative powers, that indeed the plunge into chaos is necessary for overcoming the outworn "truths" of a dead past. Douglas Robillard, one of these critics, thus writes of the process of pilgrimage Aiken records in his Preludes:

> The process of definition is to destroy the custom-made answers and evasions and to put in their place the honest recognition that however plain and disastrous the truth may be, once it is accepted it releases the angelic and nobler quality of man from the bindings of his terror.[3]

Robillard has written of Aiken's use in his early poetry of a diabolical realm that the poet accepts when he plunges into his own inner chaos. But in writing of the Preludes he notes the discovery of an "angelic order of feeling and knowledge" which "appears again and again as symbols of what man can reach."[4] Robillard is here describing what I have in another work described as the shamanic process that Aiken undergoes in order to encounter brief visions of that element Mircea Eliade calls the sacred.[5] Eliade describes in his studies of myth and shamanism the process of life, death, and rebirth as the essential action of the quest myth, or pilgrimage as this world-wide story is often called. This myth, or story, records the breakthrough of a creative energy Eliade calls in his many volumes "the sacred." Eliade writes

---

[3]Douglas Robillard, *Essays in Arts and Sciences* III, 1 (May 1974), 15.
[4]Ibid., 14.
[5]See my book *The Writer as Shaman: The Pilgrimages of Conrad Aiken and Walker Percy* (Macon: Mercer University Press, 1986).

that "the myth constitutes a 'knowledge' which is esoteric, not only because it is secret and is handed on during the course of an initiation but also because the 'knowledge' is accompanied by a magico-religious power."[6] For Eliade this power is experienced not only by shamans and mythic heroes but by artists, whose creative power is itself the result of encountering on a journey the destructive powers that always threaten the pilgrim, or mythic quester. As the quest continues, the quester encounters creative powers which express themselves as forces springing from a core in the unconscious that C. G. Jung usually called the Self but sometimes referred to as Great Man or Cosmic man or hero, to use Joseph Campbell's term. The activation of this core, symbolized by what Jung called the archetype of the mandala, is also accompanied, as Robillard has noted, by an awareness of creative power which seems to appear from without in angelic imagery. Thus Eliade writes of the artist as we know him in world civilizations in which old-fashioned shamans are no longer to be found: "[I]t is primarily the artists who represent the genuine creative forces of a civilization or a society. Through their creation the artists can anticipate what is to come. . . in other sectors of social or cultural life."[7] But how the artist derives this creative power is a mystery to many modern commentators on the arts.

For Harold Bloom creative power is achieved when the artist, wrestling with the text of a precursor, overcomes a fear, or anxiety, relating to his inevitable rewriting of the precursor's work. This aspect of Aiken's struggle to overcome threatening literary powers of the past in order to find his own literary strength can indeed be explained in Bloom's terms as we see, for instance, in *The Breaking of the Vessels*. Yet it is not only with precursors but with literary comrades that one must struggle. For instance, Pound's rabbinical qualities threatened Aiken's own gift as a rabbi (teacher) of the gnosis of modernism. And Eliot the man and the poet seemed at times so threatening that Aiken calls him Tsetse, that is, the one who castrates by putting to sleep. Also, in Bloom's meaning of the anxiety of influence, Aiken felt threatened by the musical tradition of Romanticism, even while he avails himself of it, and he denies its power over him while continuing to use musical parallels throughout his whole career. Above all, Aiken, to overcome its powerful influence on him, must deconstruct Christian theology and that rhetoric of the West that sprang from it. Thus he wrote two of the most famous deconstructive lines of modern poetry in *Preludes for Memnon*

---

[6]Mircea Eliade, *Myth and Reality* (New York: Harper and Row, 1963), 14-15.
[7]Ibid., 10.

(LVI), in which he seconds the deconstructive efforts of two children of French symbolism, Rimbaud and Verlaine: "And let us then take godhead by the neck--/ And strangle it, and with it, rhetoric" (*CP*, 565).

What Rimbaud and Verlaine seek to do and what Aiken seconds them in is what I take to be Jacques Derrida's chief deconstructive philosophy as described by Jonathan Culler: "Derrida is working, rather, to describe a general process through which texts undo the philosophical system to which they adhere by revealing its rhetorical nature."[8] Derrida's philosophy of deconstruction, Culler goes on, sets itself against semiotics: "Deconstruction enjoys announcing the impossibility of the semiotic activity."[9] Thus, Culler says, semiotics is "the logical culmination of what Jacques Derrida calls the 'logocentrism' of Western culture: the rationality which treats meanings as concepts or logical representations."[10] Culler believes that Derrida's works are at once a product of semiotics and an attempt to transcend them. The same, in a sense, may be said of Aiken if the term semiotics is extended to include the rhetorical and logical structure on which Western civilization rests. Like Derrida, Aiken is attacking the process of centering the mind on logical structures. In doing so Aiken is not denying the validity of logic or its structures because the lines that precede his seconding of Verlaine's statement to Rimbaud, "We must take rhetoric and wring its neck!" are these:

> Order in all things, logic in the dark;
> Arrangement in the atom and the spark;
> Time in the heart and sequence in the brain--
> Such as destroyed Rimbaud and fooled Verlaine. (*CP*, 565)

Even while overthrowing the products of Western logocentrism--godhead and rhetoric--Aiken is proclaiming the existence of time and order, thus reminding us of his continuing use throughout his work of musical parallels; but, at the same time, the logic he proclaims is not the worn-out logical statements of a dying civilization but rather a hidden logic that is at once orderly *and* destructive as well as being extremely deceptive.

---

[8]Jonathan Culler, *The Pursuit of Signs: Semiotics, Literature, Deconstruction* (Ithaca: Cornell University Press, 1981), 41.
[9]Ibid., 43.
[10]Ibid., 4.

Aiken's pilgrimage then can be seen as one moving through a deconstructive period--or "self- unwinding" as he called it--in order to encounter a new vision of the mysterious creative order of the universe. This vision, or rather series of small visions, is shamanic in nature in that it brings with it that "magical" quality Aiken felt the artist must always have to be a true artist. The artist struggles with the texts of the precursors and the comrades, but the struggle to be meaningful in artistic terms must involve a breakthrough into the magical powers of the self, the recovery of what Eliade calls the sacred. And behind the struggle in the Bloomian sense with literary texts is the early, half-forgotten struggle with the castrating voice of the father and the sensuous Lorelei voice of the incestuous aspect of the mother, continued by the perilous lovers that follow the mother. Like Bloom, Aiken would inevitably turn to Freud as an initiating figure. But unlike Bloom he would not consider Freud the only initiating figure. The quester, Aiken believed, is in our time initiated by several figures, but the initiatory figures only stand at the beginning of the quest. The pilgrim must eventually go alone on his journey to find creativity.

Two initiatory figures are central to the development of Conrad Aiken: Freud and Santayana. Without them, Aiken could never have taken his plunge into his own inner chaos, the event that really marks the beginning of his poetic pilgrimage. As a young man who had suffered far more by the time he was twenty-one than anybody he knew, Aiken had to have the hope offered by Freud that there was a way through psychic dislocation to a mature sexuality and to what Freud came to see as the goal of his method of aiding psychic growth that he called psychoanalysis: the development of the total love life. As one who had suffered deep frustrations in his early life as child, friend, and lover, Aiken was drawn to believe in Freud's promise that the total love life of the individual could be developed through Freud's process of making the unconscious conscious. Aiken's early poetry is largely a delving into his own unconscious mind in order to discover hidden images of pain and destruction, making conscious to himself and others like him the explosive Oedipal and castrating impulses that were to be found in the modern psyche. But for Aiken the Freudian method of psychoanalysis was not enough on which to base a life pilgrimage. Philosophical and religious needs, partly innate and partly inherited, pushed the young Aiken toward acceptance of another guide who could satisfy both needs.

Santayana as teacher and friend had shown Aiken the possibility of a new modernist philosophical poetry that had religious significance, even to the point of taking the place for many of lost religions. The full significance of psychology, philosophy, and religion in Aiken's development must be reserved for chapters devoted to each subject; but what is important here is the initiatory role of Freud and Santayana in aiding a poet whose quest was essentially that of earlier shamans. In primitive societies, as Eliade and others have noted, the shaman-to-be undergoes a testing by both inner and outer demons, which often leads to sickness and even to insanity. Traditionally, the shaman is accepted as such if he can recover from his sickness. The shaman-to-be is only encountering in himself the sickness that is in everyone in his tribe. Overcoming the demons that cause sickness means finding in himself the hidden power of creativity that makes possible both his recovery and his work for the tribe as a full-fledged shaman. Aiken possessed only a vague idea of his role as modern shaman, but he advanced boldly to the task, aided by the belief instilled in him by Freud and Santayana that he could achieve the rewards granted to those who overcame psychic illness, which were renewed love and a renewed vision of cosmic harmony.

One of the greatest acts of deconstruction in the creative life of Aiken was his plunge into his own unconscious mind to encounter forces of both psychic and sexual disintegration. Jacques Derrida in answering a question after a speech in 1985 thus defined the leading movement in the literary criticism of the eighties: "Deconstruction is decomposition."[11] Deconstruction, of course, is many things to the different critics working in this particular vineyard; but, for its leading philosopher, Derrida, it must include, at bottom, an acceptance of decomposition. For Aiken the basic acceptance of decomposition was his submission of himself to the destructive forces he records in the poetic works he groups under the title *The Divine Pilgrim*. But even as he accepts the deconstructing process within himself, Aiken seeks, for himself as a student of Santayana and Freud, the inevitable process of reconstruction. In *The Divine Pilgrim* the powers of reconstruction, present in his work almost until the end of his career, are grouped around the symbol of the pilgrim whereas the powers of deconstruction emanate from the powers of the archetypal seductive woman men must continually encounter.

Ironically, it would not be Aiken but his closest artistic companion, Eliot, consciously fleeing from his unconscious, who would in poetic form present to the world the most influential single work in English of formalistic decomposition. Clearly *The Waste Land*, which Crawford tells us "echoed and parodied" *The Divine Pilgrim* was that work. Long thought by many to

---

[11]Speech given by Derrida at Georgia State University, September 25, 1985.

be an example of a French symbolist poem in English, studies of the work in the light of deconstructive criticism should in time reveal that Eliot goes far beyond French symbolism in his style and method by approaching that annihilation of form in art that Rimbaud had announced and that Stravinsky, Schonberg, Eliot, and Joyce were moving toward in the early twentieth century. Certainly Yeats, influenced as he was by French symbolism but proclaiming himself a last Romantic, saw the deconstructive elements in both *The Waste Land* and *Ulysses* and turned away for a time from these two works. As a poet, Aiken turned away from the dissolution of style that *The Waste Land* represented, but then by the thirties, so had Eliot. As a critic Aiken could accept with praises and kind understanding the major work of Eliot's first poetic phase. Even while announcing decomposition in many lines and even in whole sections of many of his poems, however, his own need was always to uphold the chief role of the poet as a seeker after new harmonies and new creative powers--that is, as a pilgrim seeking divinity. His own deeply unsettled psyche, particularly in his early years, made him seek recomposition in both style and vision, to seek new ways of bringing to the new poetry an awareness of the poet as one who advances the consciousness and conscience of his own age, becoming in effect a kind of modern shaman who would help to release renewed humans from the fetters of a dying age.

The beginning of recomposition, of a new sense of creative order and of creative release, is found in the pivotal poem "Changing Mind," which Aiken placed at the end of *The Divine Pilgrim*, saying by that action that he had in this work recorded the end of a phase of the pilgrimage that was the central fact of his life. In this poem Aiken points to the crucifixion of the pilgrim as a necessary event in the overcoming of that illusion of absolute separateness that underlies the condition of narcissism. Through the pain of separation and isolation that grew partly from the human condition but that was intensified by his early catastrophic loss, Aiken had lived with an intense feeling of loneliness. But the possibilities of discovering a quality in life Santayana had called reason and that Freud had said was love caused Aiken to search for that necessary kind of consciousness that would make awareness and acceptance of these values possible. These values Aiken in the most important of his early poems, the one that launched in 1917 his real poetic career--"Tetélestai"--associated with the archetype of the hero, that inner Self at the core of each human. *Changing Mind* begins with the protagonist being called underwater into the darkness, an act symbolic of the pilgrim entering the depths of his own soul. Within the soul he finds what Aiken in the poem's preface calls "the constituent particles of himself" (*CP*, 872). These particles are the psychic forces which he has inherited as part of every individual's racial memory, or, as Jung called it, the collective unconscious. Also underwater he finds Narcissus: "O Alba! Look! While thus Narcissus sleeps/ Under the river, and beside him keeps/ Conscious and unconscious my bright soul!" (*CP*, 281). Then a new god appears: "Out of the east/ The blue god looms and with him come new worlds" (*CP*, 281). This god is a power that comes to aid in delivering the pilgrim from the dominance of Narcissus. How this deliverance is achieved in the poem will be taken up at the conclusion of this discussion of the Symphonies because this deliverance is in effect the chief theme of these poems. But now it is necessary to look briefly at that which the pilgrim seeks to be delivered: problems caused by his intense narcissism.

Narcissus for Aiken was a power that grew from a self-love so intense that it caused the self-concept to bewitch the conscious mind, a bewitching that made impossible the ever-widening consciousness that was central to Aiken's personal religion. Narcissism, as Freud had shown, is an inevitable stage in the individual's development. For a parentless child who continually felt deprived of love the attachment to one's self-concept that became narcissism was more necessary than it was for children living in families unviolated by murder and suicide. But throughout *The Divine Pilgrim* Aiken reveals the need for displacing in the soul the god Narcissus with those deep psychic and creative powers waiting to be activated. But even deeper in the soul than Narcissus is another power that must be overcome: the dark god Mephistopheles, the figure Jung called the shadow. This shadow figure in the poem reveals himself to the protagonist as a crucified woman, symbol of wounded feminine powers in his own soul and of his own hatred of the feminine side of all of life.

Changing Mind does not deal with overcoming this side of his shadow; later in the Preludes Aiken will reveal his gradual coming to terms with the feminine, or anima aspect, of the cosmos. But at this stage of his life Aiken would record his continuing attack on Narcissus, who had to be defeated every day if the powers of the soul, bringing with them expanded consciousness, were to be released. Aiken thus tells us that everyday the pilgrim fights a giant and is defeated. Yet this daily crucifixion by the giant becomes in fact a series of victories over Narcissus. Thus the voices of the creative psychic powers cry out: "'Alas, Narcissus dead,/ Narcissus daily dead, that we may live!'" (*CP*, 287). Christ and Socrates also dwell within the poet, and they come with other figures in the poem to Golgotha, the scene of the protagonist's daily crucifixion. Though always weak and sick, the protagonist never ceases his struggle: "Daily I fight here,/ Daily I die for the Word's delight/ By the giant blow on my visible heart!" (*CP*, 287). The continuing struggle results in a flowing of both creative and visionary powers in the poet's soul. Soon he sees a new land of joy and freedom: "[W]hile I/ Dreamed that I swam, and with that swimmer came/ Into the southeast of forgotten name" (*CP*, 283). He swims with a god toward a paradise whose name he has forgotten. In one sense Aiken, like Wordsworth, was laying hold on memories of childhood joy, but like Wordsworth and other Romantic visionary poets Aiken was revealing in *Changing Mind* momentary archetypal experience, brief encounters, that is, with powers of the individual and the collective psyche. Unlike Wordsworth and other English Romantic poets Aiken in his poetry reached his deepest archetypal experience after he had passed his fortieth year. This experience is recorded in the Preludes and *Ushant.*

Yet Aiken's major poetry, which must be seen in relationship to the affirmations of *Ushant*, rests on those poems he called the Symphonies, the works largely grouped by Aiken under the title of *The Divine Pilgrim*. Frederick J. Hoffman writes that in reading these works in Aiken's arrangement in *The Divine Pilgrim* "we sense easily enough the relation they have to one another, but we can scarcely say why there should be such an abundance." [12] My own belief, already suggested, is that Aiken's intense need to break out of the shell of his narcissism, a shell necessarily erected by the poet's catastrophic early loss, drove him to a restless creativity that is only occasionally found in the deep artistic focus he would achieve in the Preludes and *Ushant*. Indeed, the two most impressive poems that rightly belong to the Symphonies, "Tetélestai" and *Changing Mind,* mark the beginning and end of the poetic effort that produced this impressive poetic cycle. With "Tetélestai" in 1917, which Jay Martin says is Aiken's "first approach to the shortening of the symphonic mode," [13] Aiken found his authentic voice with the poem that would become, along with the early minor lyric "Music I Heard with You," one of his two most anthologized poems. "Music I Heard With You" announced the continuing Aiken theme of the relationship between music and the harmony of the spheres, from which human love springs. "Tetélestai," on the other hand, announced the

---

[12] *Selected Letters of Conrad Aiken,* 84.

[13] Jay Martin, *Conrad Aiken: A Life of His Art* (Princeton: Princeton University Press, 1962), 98.

experience of chaos and nothingness that Aiken would continually record in his work. He also announced, in this autobiographical poem that evokes his father's suicide and his own suicidal impulses, two mythic themes--the awareness of the hero within every human being and the Christ within his soul, both of which he reveals in *Changing Mind* and the Preludes. The significance of this poem as a part of Aiken's religious vision I will discuss later, but clearly it states an acceptance of a suffering leading to new life that, in *Changing Mind*, Aiken reveals as a necessary element in the psychic growth of the individual. In between these two works, which remain landmarks in the poet's career, we find in the Symphonies a group of poems that prepare the way for major poetic effort of the Preludes.

Hoffman, Martin, and others have analyzed in detail the individual Symphonies, yet the mythic significance of the works remain obscure to many Aiken readers. For Hoffman, comparing Wallace Stevens and Aiken, these poems "leap audaciously (hysterically) into regions and myths which startle by their obscurity without satisfying their purpose."[14] The primary theme in all the poems is the psychic dislocation caused by the necessary shell of narcissism that, because of the poet's continuing need for self-love in an alienating environment, can be put aside only gradually and with such small measures of pain that the psyche will not be drowned in confusion. The myths used by Aiken in the Symphonies, obscure though some of them are, constitute fragments of what James Joyce called the monomyth, that perennial story of the growth of the human psyche to a maturity that will be accompanied by the love and acceptance of all existence, both good and evil, harmony and chaos. These poems reflect the growing maturity achieved by one who has begun to experience that expanded consciousness that Aiken believed formed the basis of all religions. Through this expanded consciousness, first experienced by the poet functioning as shaman, humanity is moved into deeper levels of understanding and emotional awareness.

What the poet of the Symphonies lacks above all, however, is a profound plunge into his own psyche, one that would bring forth the kind of understanding and awareness he was seeking. The reason is that Aiken in the Symphonies chiefly concentrates on his own fragmented self, which in the necessary condition of the beginning mythic quester who, because of his narcissism, alternately adores and hates himself, adoring because he has little else to adore and hating because he falls short of its own image of what it

---

[14]Hoffman, 112.

would be like to be. Above all, the fragmented ego suffers from a painful isolation that is in fact a form of solipsism. For Robert Langbaum the problem of the fragmented ego bound up in a solipsist-narcissist ego is part of the great modern problem of the search for identity. Drawing on the researches of Christopher Lasch, Erik Erickson, and the creative works of D. H. Lawrence and W. B. Yeats, Langbaum thus states this problem:

> The solipsist-narcissist syndrome defines the main problem of identity treated by literature since the romanticists. On the one hand, there is the need for a strong individuality that can reject old values and create new ones, that can create its own organization of the world. On the other hand, there is the danger that such an individuality will make a world of itself. The solution, as formulated by Lawrence and Erik Erikson, is to maintain a strong ego open to convictions.[15]

The great question for all modern writers is what kind of "convictions," to use Langbaum's term, the "strong ego" maintains. Early in his career Aiken sought the connection traditionally called love, a power that seeks the good of the other, but in the Symphonies we find connections that destroy the two people connected. Thus many forms of sexual lust, including sadomasochism, are dealt with in several of the Symphonies. The early and middle poetry of both Eliot and Aiken contains a persistent concern with various aspects of sexuality. The two had collaborated in their college days on the pornographic "King Bolo" poems, and Peter Ackroyd reports that as late as 1927 Eliot was sending to Aiken "further Bolovian stanzas of an obscure character."[16] For Ackroyd, Eliot's covert poetic libertinism, like his more public asceticism, were ways "of assuaging or defying the meaninglessness of the universe."[17] Eliot and Aiken both had periodic bouts with the void of modern meaninglessness, but there was more than the void to be assuaged and defied. Unlike Eliot, who turned away from Freud's sexual analysis, Aiken in the Symphonies uses Freud and the trappings of Gothic romance to deal with sexual agonies that grow out of the strong sense of isolation and its accompanying loneliness. Sex is, for Aiken, an attempt

---

[15]Robert Langbaum, *The Mysteries of Identity* (Chicago: University of Chicago Press, 1982), 7.

[16]Peter Ackroyd, *T. S. Eliot: A Life* (New York: Simon and Schuster, 1984), 165.

[17]Ibid., 169.

to break out of the shell of isolation, but the result is not so much an encounter with the pleasure principle as it is with the destructive energies of overpowering females.

In such long poems as *The Charnel Rose* (1917) and *The Jig of Forslin* (1916) he records the adventures of the fragmented ego's encounter with woman as goddess and as temptress. The goddess is one of the symbols of Eros, but the witch-temptress stands for, in Freudian terminology, the fixation of the libido on the image of lust. In his early poems there are glimpses of the goddess, but the poet is often more concerned with the withdrawal of the ego into phantasies of sexual pleasure. These phantasies in turn lead to dreams of lust and horror, of manias and vampires that make up, for instance, part three of *The Jig of Forslin*. Bewitchment by images that are contemplated at first with pleasure and later with possessiveness and hate occurs regularly in Aiken's work. Aiken seems to indicate in his work that all bewitchment goes back to narcissism and to possession by the parent of the opposite sex. Thus Aiken links narcissism to the Oedipus complex.

In *Priapus and the Pool* (1922) Aiken shows a man bound by a possessive sex drive represented by Priapus, the classical god of male procreative power. The poet thus reveals the connection between lust and the narcissistic lover who has fallen in love with his own image in a pool. The poem ends with the pilgrim finally seeing the true nature of the desired woman who, while destroying others, is caught up in her own narcissism. She is Medusa: "For she could not see/ The world she turned to stone and ash./ Only herself she saw ."[18] In recognizing the witch who has tempted him in many guises, the pilgrim cries out his rejection:

> You, whose beauty I abhor--
> Out of my brain
> Take back your voice that lodges there in pain,
> Tear out your thousand golden roots
> That thrust their tentacles in my heart
> But bear no fruits. (*CP*, 396)

The witch herself is isolated and in her loneliness would possess and devour; for this reason her touch bears no fruit but turns to stone the pilgrim who looks too long. The possessive love of witch and vampire is soul-destroying lust and not the fruit-bearing love that accompanies psychic

---

[18]Frederick J. Hoffman, *Conrad Aiken* (New York: Twayne Publishers, 1962), 112.

growth. But it is not enough simply to denounce evil; to overcome it one must have help from the higher beings who come to the aid of the pilgrim. In *Priapus and the Pool* these figures appear to the poet as lovers from Atlantis, a symbol of a lost paradise where love was always giving and receiving and not, as in our fallen world, a mixture of joy and cruel possessiveness. The speech of the divine lovers is filled with the language of that higher life toward which the divine pilgrim journeys:

> Thereafter, where they go or come,
> They will be silent; they have heard
> Out of the infinite of the soul
> An incommunicable word;
>
> Thereafter, they are as lovers who
> Over an infinite brightness lean:
> "It is Atlantis!" All their speech;
> "To lost Atlantis have we been." (*CP*, 394)

In the Symphonies Aiken, pursuing the trappings of a Romantic supernaturalism, shows his protagonist encountering female witches and vampires who threaten both life and immortal soul. But in using the mythic knowledge he had discovered in Romantic literature, Aiken depicts the protagonist calling on the powers of creativity for help. He can do this because he is able to affirm a basic cosmic unity that protects all those who believe in it. Behind images borrowed from late and decadent Romanticism Aiken was using knowledge gleaned from his studies of depth psychology. A sense of cosmic unity sprang from his study of Santayana and from the Unitarian heritage that, unlike Eliot, he never cast away. But also this cosmic sense is expressed in terms of what C. G. Jung called the most basic of all archetypes, the mandala. To escape the bewitching and destructive powers of vampirism the mandala must continually be affirmed by the pilgrim. The dark powers threaten to annihilate the soul, which is tempted to withdraw into the remembrance of past oedipal pleasures. But to withdraw completely would be to lose the creative powers of the unconscious mind (in Jungian teaching) and to fail to achieve full sexuality (in the Freudian doctrine). By adopting the attitude of the mythic quester (or divine pilgrim, as he calls this figure) the protagonist, who is both a Unitarian and a modern depth psychologist, pushes past the threatening and destructive powers in order to experience moments of both psychic and sexual renewal.

Aiken thus deals with problems of narcissism and sexual obsession in mythic terms as well as in psychological terms. Freud had declared the importance of the dream, and Aiken had followed him by seeking insights into his own psyche through a study of his own dreams. Bad dreams for Aiken could reveal the dangerous powers that threatened the psyche while dreams of triumph showed the progress of the pilgrim in overcoming both narcissism and destructive sexual obsessions. Aiken's most powerful poem dealing with the overcoming of narcissism, *Changing Mind,* was placed at the end of *The Divine Pilgrim* as if to announce the end of one phase of Aiken's poetic career. It was, as Aiken once told me, based on one of his own dreams, and in this poem Aiken spells out the meaning of suffering in the life of the pilgrim. Both suffering and death are necessary tests in that they require the pilgrim to affirm cosmic unity in order to overcome the illusion of basic separateness that results in narcissism, which is a worship of one's own image resulting from the despair at feeling unloved or unwanted.

The pilgrim, after plunging into the soul, discovers a creative psychic power called a god, which aids him in overcoming Narcissus, that symbol of the bewitching image that traps the pilgrim's creative energies, called by Jung the shadow. The shadow, as Aiken tells us in the Preludes, is the final psychic enemy to be overcome. In *Changing Mind* the pilgrim fights and is defeated by a giant who symbolizes the shadow. Yet through crucifixion the pilgrim in *Changing Mind* and later poems rises to continuing victories over the shadow. Thus Aiken as mythic poet and pilgrim identifies himself with the man who fights everyday for the freedom of his creative soul in order to experience a continually expanding consciousness. Thus he reminds us of Goethe in his *Faust,* who considered the daily fight for individual freedom the most important human act.

With "Tetélestai" in 1917, Aiken began to define his own psychic illness and his continuing effort through pilgrimage, to achieve a measure of psychic health and a deeper vision of the lost paradise of his childhood. After his suicide attempt in 1932, he would proceed confidently forward with the major poems of his life, the Preludes; in these he recorded his continuing struggle with Narcissus and Mephistopheles; but, above all else, he proclaimed his visionary awareness of the fruitful creative powers to be found in the human psyche. In his best work after 1917 he would record momentary encounters with the joys of a nearly forgotten childhood before he was possessed by images of his two violently slain parents, suddenly discovered in the very next room of the beloved house in Savannah. Aiken's search for deeper visions of this remembered childhood joy, as well as deeper insights into his psychic trauma, would take him through the Preludes and other poems written in the 1930s and 40s as well as through his greatest prose work, *Ushant*. He would thus record his glimpses of paradise and his growing awareness of and belief in the great pilgrimage that is possible for all human beings toward a continuing evolution of consciousness and toward that godhead itself which his grandfather Potter believed was everyone's birthright. Before I examine Aiken's greatest literary achievements, it is necessary to analyze the poet's fictional descent into his own tortured psyche, a descent rendered more profoundly than those individual descents recorded in the Symphonies.

Chapter 6

Fictional Descent into Hell

Aiken as a young man before World War I, already moving with Pound, Eliot, and others toward that fulfillment of modernism to become manifest at last in the twenties, was caught between, on one hand, the early idealism of *Earth Triumphant* and "Music I Heard With You" and, on the other, the psychological realism of *The Charnel Rose* and *The Jig of Forslin*. "Even as late 1917, after both *The Charnel Rose* and *The Jig of Forslin* had been written," Jay Martin writes, "the demarcation between Aiken's realistic and lyrical poems was still patent--as if he were compelled to move successfully from the one to the other."[1] In fact, the form of his early realistic poems, which often examined his own painful and threatened sexuality, was largely that of the almost worn out tradition of late pre-war Romanticism. But by 1917 with "Tetélestai" Aiken had in both form and vision begun to break through to a kind of modernism Eliot and Pound had achieved in "The Love Song of J. Alfred Prufrock" and "Hugh Selwyn Mauberly," poems in which both form and content point to the threatened disintegration of individuals who still maintained the validity of their own spiritual awareness, who were, in Aiken's term, still divine pilgrims.

The late Romanticism of most of the poems of *The Divine Pilgrim*, that first great cycle of Aiken poems, conceals and reveals at the same time the threats of destruction as well as the painful awareness of the agony of sexual conflicts. Poems like *John Deth* and *Changing Mind*, as I have suggested, mark the end of *The Divine Pilgrim* and the beginning of the Preludes. What Aiken needed for his own development as an artist and a pilgrim was to create a body of work that would clarify his struggle with his inner demons. In the best poems of *The Divine Pilgrim*, Aiken, using his own life, sought to work within that modernist tradition whose leaders by 1930 had become Eliot, Pound, and Joyce, a tradition that called for the elimination of the poets personality within the individual work. Thus Aiken in much of the early poetry sought to present a typical life and not his own particular life story. But in two short story collections, *Bring! Bring!* (1925) and *Costumes by Eros* (1928), and in the novel *Blue Voyage* (1927), Aiken would, in

---

[1]Jay Martin, *Conrad Aiken* (Princeton: Princeton University Press, 1962), 15.

Martin's words, "replace the Divine Pilgrim with the Man--Conrad Aiken."[2] Thus in his fiction would emerge Aiken the confessional artist.

From the beginning of his career Aiken was aware of the dangers to the artist of the immersion in confession. Can confession ever be more than autobiography?, he asked himself as a budding critic. He also asked himself why he should bother with the art of fiction and the art of poetry. In a critical note published in 1944 Aiken finally sums up in a characteristically pithy manner the meaning of his efforts to mediate between confession and art. Whit Burnett had in the early forties asked "Americas 93 Greatest Living Authors" to choose the work they thought their best. Aiken picked the story "Strange Moonlight" from *Bring! Bring!,* and gave his reasons for his choice. The story, he says, is "largely autobiographical." But "when a writer makes over, or partly makes over, his experience into a poem or story, he will then tend to forget the experience itself." The act of creation, he says, is "the act of thus formalizing and externalizing a memory." The result will be that the author will find his own experience "more accessible, and far vivider, in the artifact than in his own recollection."[3]

Presumably the reader would, through the creation of an "artifact," to use Aiken's term, experience a vividness and power he would not gain simply from a factual confession. Aiken thus had reached by 1944 a critical viewpoint that allowed him to explain how his best fiction had earlier explored the dark side of his own life while still retaining a strong sense of his role as artist.

As a fictional artist Aiken could effectively use mythic images--hell, for instance, is an image with which he opens "Strange Moonlight"--in order to evoke that power of the imagination that the confessional artist must possess if he is to be more than a chronicler of his miseries and triumphs. But also Aiken as a philosophical poet found it necessary to embody in all of his best fiction the knowledge that he had accumulated from his Harvard days with Santayana until the moment of writing a work. For instance, Martin tells us that "nearly all of his fictional works are in fact the poets "attempts to remember, by setting down, the pain he has caused both to others and to himself. In his consciousness of his failures he seeks forgiveness for them; and, more than forgiveness: the understanding which will allow him to

---

[2]Ibid., 67.

[3]Conrad Aiken, introduction to *Strange Moonlight, This is My Best* ed. Whit Burnett (New York: Halcyon House, 1944), 85.

transcend them, in life as in art."[4]   The struggle with his own inner pain and its outer manifestations would be most deeply recorded in only a handful of poems, short stories, and passages in two novels, *Blue Voyage* and *Great Circle,* Aiken's inner hell and the moments of psychic pain he knew first with his father and then with others who wounded him could be encountered only briefly in his work because of the agony of the encounter. As so often in his poetry Aiken must first call for help on some work of literature or on some familiar setting to ease the descent into the memory of personal hell.

In "Strange Moonlight," possibly Aiken's most heartfelt story but not his most powerful, the author invokes the horror stories of Poe and the beauty of Savannah and the beach twenty miles beyond the city. The theme of the descent into hell is presented in the first paragraph in terms of Poe:

> In the first place, he had filched a volume of Poes tales from his mothers bookcase, and had in consequence a delirious night in inferno. Down, down he had gone with heavy clangs about him, coiling spouts of fire licking dryly at an iron sky, and a strange companion, of protean shape and size, walking and talking beside him.[5]

Aiken's use here of Poe is an example of the role intertextuality played in his work. Without literature and art Aiken's own life would have seemed too disorderly for any kind of sane encounter. Intertextual awareness early drew Eliot and Aiken together, and not accidentally these two men were, from early in their lives, caught up in a literary awareness far deeper even than that of most modern writers. Thus Ackroyd writes that it was only in response to other poetry that Eliot could express his own deepest feelings." Eliots was thus "an imagination which went to literature for that which life could not give--a sense of order and significance, and the possibility of dramatic intensity."[6] Certainly one aspect of intertextuality, as this statement explains, is the need to find an order in art not found in life. Only those like Aiken and Eliot who early were aware of the possibilities of personal disintegration could have possessed such a great need for the ordering influence of literature. And for Aiken--as for Eliot also--a vision of nature was also

---

[4] Martin, 86.

[5] *The Collected Short Stories of Conrad Aiken* (Cleveland and New York: The World Publishing Co., 1965), 281. All subsequent references are to this volume.

[6] Peter Ackroyd, *T. S. Eliot: A Life* (New York: Simon and Schuster, 1984), 179.

necessary to give meaning to a childs too early awareness first of parental sexuality, then of approaching violence, and, finally, of a foreboding of parental destruction.

In "Strange Moonlight" a young boy encounters the death of a friend and then the combined quarreling and sexual play of his parents. Yet he is shielded by his reading of Poe and then by the invocation of nature, particularly the strangeness of moonlight, which on the return of the family from a day at the beach symbolizes the beginning of the awakening, in pain and mystery, of the boys creative powers. The release of these powers comes partly as a result of overcoming the castrating powers of the father throughout the symbolic act of burying the father in sand at the beach. The last section of the story begins: "The chief event of the afternoon was the burial of his father, who had on his bathing-suit" (*CS*, 292). And then: "How exactly like a new grave he looked." On the return from the beach to "the familiar house" all is changed: the house and the "two familiar trees" are "speeding like a fiery comet toward the worlds edge, to plunge out into the unknown and fall down and down forever" (*CS*, 294). The story ends with the awareness that "Everything was changed and ghostly" and that his young friend Caroline was in fact dead.

Part of the power of "Strange Moonlight" grows out of Aiken's remembrance of his own unconscious and clairvoyant awareness of his fathers approaching death. What he seeks to accomplish in the story is, in large part, a reconciliation both with his father and with the fact of death in all its mysterious forms. Months before his fathers death Aiken had suffered continuing abuse from a parent in the process of losing his mind. That the young Aiken should desire his fathers death for this abuse and that he should repress that desire are both actions modern psychologists have continually observed in children who have suffered as Aiken had. Also well known from many studies is the childs sense of a crushing guilt, no matter what the circumstances, when a family is shattered by divorce or something far worse, loss of a family due to the murder-suicide of the parents. The inner hell of a long continued guilt had eventually to be expunged if Aiken was to find a release from his own isolation in order to experience the renewal of his creative powers. And it is with awareness of Aiken's personal pilgrimage that the two greatest and best known stories, "Silent Snow, Secret Snow" and "Mr. Arcularis," should be viewed.

Because he knew Aiken well and had even received in a letter Aiken's own account of the degree of autobiography in his stories, we must accept, on one level at least, Martins statement that the two great stories "have only slight and peripheral relations to his [Aiken's] own experience."[7] Yet "Silent Snow, Secret Snow" and "Mr. Arcularis" represent the profoundest movements of the writers soul in relationships both to his continuing sense of guilt, his long and painful isolation, his continuing narcissism, and his efforts to move beyond that narcissism and its self-centered destructiveness. The pain and complexity of this movement of the soul was so great that Aiken, in most matters of his life the master confessionalist, could never talk about his greatest single fictional triumph, "Silent Snow, Secret Snow." I once asked Aiken, then in his late seventies, about the autobiographical background of the story, and he smiled wistfully and said, "Everybody asks me about that one." Yet knowing Aiken's psychological development as he generally reveals it in admittedly autobiographical verse and fiction, it is not hard to interpret either this story or "Mr. Arcularis." In the former the author records a growing withdrawal from reality due to the psychic pain inflicted on him within the family. The father can communicate with the son only in a harsh, castrating voice, never in the accents of love. Thus denied what was for Aiken the one great power of goodness, an all-embracing love, the child can only journey to another, imaginary world to find a love and happiness denied him in the only one he knows. It is a world of beauty with snow at its center, but it is also the world of isolation, of sleep, and finally, death. No doubt as a child in the last year of his fathers life, Aiken had been tempted to withdraw forever from the madhouse that had once been affectionately remembered as a loving family. A paradox that Aiken himself probably never fully accepted was that the death of his father was necessary to save him from either madness or death, or both. The story is valuable as a record of growing schizophrenia, but it also is an important modern story that probes the mind of a child.

The literary value of "Silent Snow, Secret Snow" resides primarily, as Frederick Hoffman suggests, in the fact that the "narrative consistently stays within the boys mind, moving with it toward his destruction, never suggesting or stating reasons or trying to probe psychologically into the boys injured spirit." And thus, Hoffman continues, the story "is a psychic scene of remarkable purity."[8] Hoffman writes of the storys "purity" in terms of the formalist aspect of the New Criticism, an aspect that would point toward the sustained intensity of the narrative, always kept within the childs mind. With the tools used by formalism, Hoffman rightly examines the care taken with

---

[7]Martin, 83.
[8]Frederick J. Hoffman, *Conrad Aiken* (New York: Twayne Publishers, 1962), 41.

the structure and the texture, particularly the diction, to render that single powerful mental and emotional effect so many readers have reported experiencing in this modern masterpiece. But a deconstructionist view of the story would also point to literary values of the work that the New Critics have neglected. These values have to do with the determination of the child to overthrow the logocentrism of the school where we first find him and then later that of his mother and father. The overthrow, sweeping in its nature, is accomplished for the sake of voyaging to a new, superior realm of existence, one both beautiful and deadly. Aiken's presentation of these two aspects of the childs newfound realm of psychic experience reminds us of the psychologist R. D. Laings belief that the schizophrenic is in fact seeking a breakthrough to a new realm of creative existence. Aiken presents this breakthrough in intertextual terms by revealing at the beginning of the story the way that the teachers description of geographical areas has springboarded the boy into his voyage of discovery.

By the end of the narrative the child is hearing not the "dead" stories of his teacher and his parents but has received a new story from the voice that has become the center of his new rarified existence: "Listen!" it said. Well tell you the last, the most beautiful and secret story--shut your eyes--it is a very small story--a story that gets smaller and smaller--it comes inward instead of opening like a flower[.]" (*CS*, 235). Like "Strange Moonlight," "Silent Snow, Secret Snow" opens with the awareness of a story about unknown regions--the tropics and the polar region--and goes on to a story that resolves psychic problems. In "Strange Moonlight" the boy is led to an unconscious acceptance of his fathers death and to a conscious belief that his friend Caroline is at last dead and that this death can be seen as meaningful in a framework that involves the sea and the moon, symbols for Aiken throughout his life of what Hoffman calls the poets "cosmic naturalism." The boys discovery of a cosmic wholeness in nature in "Strange Moonlight" is the new story that supersedes the old one that calls the individual to begin a journey. Thus the snow at the end of "Silent Snow, Secret Snow" "rose and fell like enormous whispering sea-waves, the whisper becoming louder, the laughter more numerous" (*CS*, 235).

"Mr. Arcularis," a celebrated story that was rewritten to become Aiken's one play, begins, like the two stories already discussed, with a story that sets off a vision. The ending of the story presents another world discovered, and a story set to music, "Cavalleria Rusticana," transformed from "sobbing among the palms" to "light, delight, supreme white and brightness, whirling lightness above all--and freezing-freezing-freezing... (*CS*, 53). The storys setting is what, in conclusion, Aiken calls "the ordered life of the hospital." The sound of the opera projects Mr. Arcularis beyond this logocentric world where he has temporarily lost his real self. He is plunged into a dream of taking a voyage to England ordered by his doctor, a trip that he believes will mark the beginning of a new life. He moves through an ordered Boston, past his beloved Harvard Club, where he enjoyed years of ordered pleasures, to a well ordered ship waiting to serve every reasonable demand of its passengers. Yet everywhere a strangeness surrounds Arcularis, represented above all else by the unexpected and enduring chill in the June air. Once at sea the chill never leaves him and the strangeness for him continues even as the activities of the other passengers seemed fixed in orbits: "How odd to reflect on the fixed little orbits of these things--as definite and profound, perhaps, as the orbits of the stars, and as important to God or the Absolute. There was a kind of tyranny in this fixedness, too..." (*CS*, 41). What overcomes the tyranny is a series of profound dreams that bring with them pain along with visions of the dark and cold. Voices of ordered authority reassure him: the doctor tells him he is worried and the parson tells him, "You feel guilty about something" (*CS*, 47). A woman assures him there is nothing to worry about. Images of isolation and cold continue as he hears from the ships orchestra the same strains from "Cavalleria" that had projected his mind beyond the order of the hospital. But pain and cold are finally overcome by explosion into a vision of new life:

> Forward into the untrodden! Courage, old man, and hold onto your umbrella! Have you got your garters on? Mind your hat! In no time at all well be back to Clarice with the frozen rime-feather, the time-feather, the snowflake of the Absolute, the Obsolete. If only we dont wake... if only we dont wake in that--in that--time and space... somewhere or nowhere... cold and dark. (*CS*, 53)

The new life thus briefly described is summed up as "light, delight, supreme white and brightness, whirling lightness above all--and freezing--freezing..." (*CS*, 53). Arcularis has deconstructed his logocentric, time-ridden world and has found a new one in which the Absolute is obsolete. Thus a talisman called the "time-feather" opens the door to pure being where the opposites of cold and dark, God and man no longer exist. Yet to achieve this deconstruction of a logocentric world that has denied his psychic pain, the root cause of his physical pain, he has had to die. The last words of the story belong to a logocentric world represented by the "ordered life of the hospital," where the death of Mr. Arcularis is marked only by "a pause, a brief flight of unexchanged comment" (*CS*, 53).

Like "Silent Snow, Secret Snow," the story of Mr. Arcularis shows the deconstructive reaction to an order that denies the souls suffering as that of a final withdrawal, taking the form of schizophrenia (in which the individual creates his own world) and, as in the latter story, a physical death seen as both escape and adventure. Aiken's handling of the twin problems of total insanity and death is very much in the Romantic tradition going back to Chatterton and Goethe, who deal with the problem of the sensitive poet withdrawing from a world whose order denies the reality perceived by the imagination. The same theme is found in modern literature extending from the Naturalism of Zola, Dreiser, or Dos Passos to modern Romantics like Rilke or Kafka. It might be the predominant theme of the stories in *Bring! Bring!*, appearing in the 1920s, when works by Hemingway and Fitzgerald were presenting the theme successfully in what might have been the last truly Romantic decade. As Balakian tells us, the symbolist poetry of the late 1890s was largely death-oriented, representing as it so often did the visions of overly sensitive poets who increasingly saw beneath ordered surfaces of society a kind of hell. T. S. Eliots *The Waste Land,* written in the symbolist tradition, presents London as a kind of hell in which the poet descends into fear and uncertainty just as two of Aiken's significant poetic works of the twenties--*Priapus and the Pool* and *John Deth: A Metaphysical Legend*--deal with the plunge into the terrors of the soul and the encounter with death. Eliot and Aiken both suggest at the end of these poems the possibility of a release from the terrors of a world presented as being evil. The late Romantic view--which Eliot and Aiken both shared in part-- pointed toward such examples of withdrawal as aestheticism, drugs, insanity, and death. All that we know of the lives of Eliot and Aiken suggests that the two men sometimes hovered on the boundaries of sanity. It is also clear that Aiken was pursued into the early thirties with strong suicidal impulses.

Eliot, Aiken, and many other literary artists of the twenties who had inherited the symbolist tradition with its late Romantic decadence felt the strong need to descend into both the inner hell of their lives and the outer destructiveness of a civilization still caught up in the disruptions of World War I. In this civilization they found a paralyzing order that threatened creativity as well as a strong death wish still left over from the catastrophes of war and large scale revolution. Yet in his two best stories-- "Silent Snow, Secret Snow" and "Mr. Arcularis"--Aiken presents the plunge into death as an escape both from a logocentric order and the terrors arising from personal and social disintegration. What the endings of the two stories both suggest is a death that promises not simply escape but a vision of a more creative life. Nevertheless, the stories represent an end of a decadent Romanticism that often turned to physical death as a way out of inner and outer tortures that sensitive people, particularly artists, felt they had to endure in a world that denied their worth. What Aiken's first novel, *Blue Voyage*, would accomplish is the move into the modernist quest for a series of symbolic deaths followed by spiritual rebirth that Mircea Eliade, Joseph Campbell, and other mythographers call the essence of the mythic quest.

In the examples of Santayana and Freud, Aiken had even before 1920 discovered the possibilities of transforming inner terrors into a series of symbolic deaths followed by new creativity, but in the example of Joyces *Ulysses* he found a poet who could apply the mythic vision to the logocentric paralysis and the disorder of modern life. In *Ulysses* Joyce at once deconstructed the old novel of Western civilization, and, as T. S. Eliot noted as early as 1922 when the work was published, Joyce had found in myth a principle of order for fiction that was based on artistic vision. In the very same year Aiken began *Blue Voyage* and continued writing it in an on-and-off process until 1926. In spite of certain obvious similarities between *Ulysses* and *Blue Voyage*, Martin correctly points out that "*Blue Voyage* was only slightly influenced by the methods and psychological schemata of Joyce and Dorothy Richardson." Yet at the same time he quotes Aiken's statement that "*Ulysses* was a landmark in my life" without showing why this should be.[9] What Joyce really taught Aiken was the possibility of encountering the hellish aspects of himself and the diabolical side of the world around him without the necessity of a total withdrawal into either death or insanity. The spirit of Joyces *Ulysses* is what Aiken absorbed, and it was in that spirit that he became fully a modernist in that major tradition which includes many of the greatest names of this century--Joyce, Pound, Yeats, Eliot, Mann, Hesse, Gide, Valéry, Joyce, Aiken,, Hemingway, Pasternak. This mainstream modernism is that of the survivors, those who suffer the inner and outer wasteland and yet keep on moving through it, sustained in that journey by what Joyce called the epiphany, the small vision that betokens the mythic possibilities of continuing personal renewal. Inevitably, these mainstream modernists included much that was autobiographical in their work because their theme was the continuing quest

---

[9]Martin, 94.

of the individual to achieve a creative relationship with fellow human beings in a disintegrating civilization.

In *Blue Voyage* Aiken turns from the partial autobiography of most of his short stories to full-scale confession. Thus he writes in 1965 of *Blue Voyage*: "Naturally, therefore, the novel is autobiographical: every bit of it is based on fact."[10] Yet earlier in the same essay he writes:

> And, of course, the vision was the thing, as it was and always will be: without that no amount of observation, or cataloging, or mere naming... can ever add up to any sort of totality of response to the universe with which we are faced, outer and inner.[11]

Martin did not have the benefit of the above definition of the modernist novel that Joyce, Aiken, and so many others would be writing after 1920. Yet Martin in writing that "Aiken was trying to fuse the confessional with the aesthetic novel, to move simultaneously in two directions" could not grasp that Aiken had turned autobiography into an aesthetic through his fictional rendition of the series of small visions (epiphanies) that his protagonist Demarest undergoes in order to achieve enough of a "totality of response" to the universe "to allow him to survive."[12] These visions enable him to accept the death of his old life and to find a new existence in which his narcissism and his inferiority complex no longer impede his psychic development.

Demarest sets out, like Arcularis, on an ocean voyage with the awareness of his own personal disintegration staring him in the face. Arcularis is unable to relate his personal suffering, symbolized by music from *Cavelleria Rusticana*, to a logocentric world that denies emotional choices; and like so many Romantics he chooses personal decomposition. Demarest, on the other hand, projects his Oedipal-narcissistic fixation onto the beloved Cynthia, who has chosen someone else. At the same time he dissolves in large part his inferiority complex by seeing that his image of himself as successful writer has nothing to do with his personal quest for a meaningful existence. His problems, he discovers on the voyage, are within himself, within the area traditionally called the soul. Demarest is aided in his quest by Silberstein, an American chewing gum salesman, who plays the role of initiator for the

---

[10]Preface, *3 Novels* (New York: McGraw Hill Book Company, 1965), iii.
[11]Ibid., ii.
[12]Martin, 94.

quester. Silberstein, an amateur psychoanalyst, is also Freud, for Aiken the modern initiatory priest who probes both consciousness and the unconscious mind, and by doing so stimulates dreams and intellectual insights so that repressed emotions and sexual power can emerge. At last Demarest learns that his Oedipal fixation on Cynthia is a flight from a feared sexuality, and by the end of the novel he begins to experience a healthy sexuality. He also learns this truth from another depth psychologist, Alfred Adler: the will to power, along with the adulation it brings, springs from low self-esteem. Adler thought that creative human interaction alone could free the quester from depression and the death wish to which it leads. But with all his personal suffering Demarest, before he yields to the death wish, remembers that it is not erotic love or fame as a writer that he really believes in but rather the lifelong quest for love and self-knowledge. Images of love and artistic success had pushed themselves to the center of his consciousness because of his inability to face his own logocentric family life and the emotional deprivation he knew in it. Like *Ulysses*, then, *Blue Voyage* is a novel of both quest and initiation. Joyces Bloom became a symbol for Aiken of that sense of personal worth every human being craves. Demarest finally sees that only the search for his inner self can bring him a sense of his own worth and an ability to give and receive love.

Blue Voyage is far more than a psychological thriller with pat solutions for the modern malaise. As I will later suggest, Aiken's psychological views are deeply interrelated with his philosophical and religious assumptions. Freud, for instance, is Socrates in modern dress, the initiatory figure who points the way to self-knowledge, that value necessary for meaningful existence. Silberstein, the wandering Jew, also reminds Demarest of his deepest connection with a Judeo-Christian past he thought he had lost. Demarest at last calls on his inherited past and invokes Jesus as one whose life was centered in love. Demarests need for love overshadows everything else in his life and the cry of the heart for love is answered. But the answer, best understood in relationship to Aiken's philosophy and his personal religion, grows out of his small visionary glimpses into himself. Of one of those glimpses, Demarest, as he begins to find enough wholeness within himself to go on living, says: "We accept everything. We deny nothing. We are, in fact, imagination: not completely, for then we should be God; but almost completely. Perhaps, in time, our imagination *will* be complete."[13]

---

[13]Conrad Aiken, *Blue Voyage* (New York: Scribners, 1928), 250.

In *Blue Voyage* Aiken has continued his analysis of the fragmented psyches searching at first for just enough stability to avoid disintegration. This is the same individual who is at the center of those "Symphonies" of the twenties like *Senlin, Punch, Priapus and the Pool, The Pilgrimage of Festus.* In these poems the descent into the hell of inner being mainly concerns the kind of decadent late Romantic individualism that was a side of Aiken in the twenties. But in *Blue Voyage* and the best stories of this period--and they are only a handful with the rest never getting beneath the surface of life--the late Romantic begins to wither way, to be replaced by another figure, Demarest in *Blue Voyage* and then Andy Cather in *Great Circle.* To get to that new figure who can face the worst part of himself and then find the love and self-knowledge to enter a new life, Aiken must slough off a part of himself that dreads the light of vision. But Aiken's desperation, mirrored so well in Demarest, demands a new life if death itself is to be escaped.

One probably must conclude that Aiken would not have dug deeply into his unconscious mind to find what Peterson calls the music of chaos unless he had actually been forced to by personal necessity. That necessity came again in the early thirties when the poet was tormented by his guilt and dismay at losing his first wife as well as by the psychic torture that grew out of his second marriage. There was also the continuing failure of his work to attract much attention, the temporary desertion by Eliot, the insanity of Fletcher, the alcoholism of his adopted son Malcolm Lowry, all of which led Aiken to make the suicide attempt that his continuing depression must have, in a hundred inner voices, urged him to make. Out of that pain came Aiken's second significant novel, *Great Circle,* the book Freud kept on his waiting room table for patients to read because the founder of psychoanalysis rightly saw in it an honest attempt of a desperately wounded man to go on living. But, like *Blue Voyage, Great Circle* is not an autobiographical record, though it begins as that. It is a work of psychological insight held together by Aiken's dreams and interior monologues. Of the process that leads to the revival of Aiken's protagonist, a leading scholar of Freudianism in modern literature, Frederick J. Hoffman, writes:

Perhaps it is too much to expect that this case of Andrew Cather will prove to be a great novel; but it is a much underrated work. Seen in the perspective of Aiken's other work, and after a fresh reading of it, what appears at first impression to be frantic images are acceptable as one of the most precise descriptions of the imagery of fright and terror.[14]

This is a just statement that most Aiken admirers would probably agree with. Yet Hoffman fails to put his finger on the books chief problem. Artistically it is not all of a piece because it represents at once what Aiken achieved in his three or four best short stories and what he brought forth in those lesser stories, which were meant to have an easy appeal for readers of the popular fiction of the period between the wars. Thus parts of the book are clearly dated as are most of Aiken's stories, but the successful dreams and monologues in *Great Circle* remain artistically significant because they consist of powerful images of "fright and terror," to use Hoffmans terms, which were drawn out of the depths of Aiken's unconscious. Malcolm Cowley is more specific about the value of these individual passages in his reminiscence, where, referring to *Great Circle,* he says that it "contains a brilliant, drunken, self-revealing monologue that Freud admired."[15] Add to this monologue Aiken's dreams and other interior thoughts, and we have powerful material not integrated into a refined fictional form like Aiken's best stories and *Blue Voyage.* Still the power remains; and this power, as Cowley says, is often linked with "the climax of Aiken's stories" and is "the true theme of his autobiography, *Ushant*": self-discovery.[16] To be more precise, the great theme of Aiken's best work is the discovery of hidden aspects of himself that in fact must be revealed if he is to continue living. But the most important aspect of self-discovery in the great poems of the thirties, the Preludes, and in *Ushant* is Aiken's encounter with that center within the psyche that he sometimes calls the Self and other times calls the god within. Encounter with this center gives the individual, he tells us, the power to overcome ones inherited fear, guilt, and self-hatred. This most important of all self- discoveries Aiken could not present in fiction because, at his best, he sought to use stories and novels as an artistic means of presenting his own encounter with the hellish aspects within both himself and the world around him. To understand Aiken's major efforts at passing through these hellish conditions, efforts in fact of exorcism, we must examine works that belong to what I have called Aiken's apocalyptic period.

---

[14]Hoffman, 48.

[15]Malcolm Cowley, "Conrad Aiken: From Savannah to Emerson," *The Southern Review,* XI, no. 2 (Spring, 1975), 2.

[16]Ibid.

Those readers who are primarily concerned with Aiken as novelist may well object to what might seem to be a slighting of his other three novels, *Conversations* (1940), in part a satire of New York Bohemianism based on his acquaintance with Max Bodenheim, is the sort of novel of manners Aiken had small experience in writing but which still reveals, as Mary Martin Rountree says, "the depth of his commitment to his original concept of his role as a servant-example in the evolution of consciousness." She goes on to suggest that this minor but important novel "represents the final step in the completion of his own great circle in fiction, the step that would ultimately lead to *Ushant*.[17] *A Heart for the Gods of Mexico* (1939) is another matter. This book contains themes important to Aiken--the death of a young girl, the awareness of the totality of America, and the meaning of Mexico to the American experience. The problem is that Aiken simply had not prepared himself properly for writing this novel and did not, because at the time his deepest energies were devoted to the Preludes and other poetry, have sufficient artistic power to bring off what he was attempting. *King Coffin* (1935) was another matter altogether. This book, once used in a psychology course at Harvard, is in fact a kind of case study. Thus it is more a work of the intellect than of the artistic imagination. What it says throws light on important aspects of the problem of narcissism and is probably an indirect way of apologizing to himself and others for his sometimes dreadful behavior. Being a work of the mind, it lacks artistic power; yet it does make an important statement about Aiken's narcissism and narcissism generally, one that I will analyze in a later chapter devoted to Aiken and depth psychology.

What Aiken achieved with his fictional descent into his own inner hell he himself summed up in his preface to *3 Novels*, written in his seventies. This preface reveals that Aiken's critical powers and his understanding of his own work had actually increased with age. After making clear that at the writing of *Blue Voyage* he was "steeped in the psychoanalytical movement and its concepts, notably those of Freud, Ferenczi and Adler," he states what the hero of *Blue Voyage* accomplished, which is also precisely what Aiken himself accomplished in his own lifes pilgrimage: "Here was the artist-hero-servant in a new predicament: he could understand his neurosis, and then proceed to create with it, on the one hand, while he analyzed both

---

[17]Mary Martin Rountree, "Conrad Aiken's Heroes: Portraits of the Artist as a Middle-Aged Failure," *Studies in the Literary Imagination*, XIII, no. 2 (Fall, 1980), 80.

the neurosis and himself away with the other."[18] By analyzing himself away Aiken meant that he had deconstructed his own self-concept--had, that is, overcome his narcissistic fixation on his image as a significant writer in order to encounter his creative powers. *Changing Mind* recorded the beginning of this deconstructive process, but *Blue Voyage* did not literally analyze away fully the poets image fixation (Aiken thus overstates the case) but rather his best fiction continues the process begun earlier in what he would call his divine pilgrimage. It was a necessary process to get himself in touch with the creative powers that would enable him to discover an apocalyptic awareness in the new decade of the thirties. Out of this awareness would emerge his greatest work, the Preludes and *Ushant,* both of which would continue the deconstructing process, that is, the overcoming of neurosis and narcissistic fixations and with this process the concomitant discovery of deeper creative energies.

---

[18]Preface, *3 Novels*, ii.

.

Chapter 7

Apocalypse: *Ushant* and the Preludes

The intellectual historian Franklin L. Baumer tells us that the word "apocalypse" literally means "an unveiling or disclosure of the future" and that the apocalyptic consciousness has been mounting in intensity since the second half of the nineteenth century when individuals like Burckhardt, Nietzsche, and Dostoevski were predicting the collapse of Western civilization. The apocalyptic spirit pervades Conrad Aiken's best work from the time he began his major poetry cycle, which he called the Preludes, until he published his autobiography *Ushant* in 1952 during his sixty-third year. The apocalyptic spirit, Baumer notes, is often extremely pessimistic, connected as it is with "crisis thinking," which "feeds upon the wars and rumors of war, the concentration camps, the tyranny, the economic and social dislocation . . . and the big state, party, business labor union, the ultimate military weapon, which reduces the individual to insignificance.'"[1] Aiken by 1931 was mired in the general pessimism of serious writers and had by then accepted the significance for himself and the Western world of the economic collapse called the Great Depression and the growing fear of large wars yet to come. Aiken also suffered more than ever from the failure to make a large name for himself in modern letters. Thus his fictional heroes in *Blue Voyage, Great Circle,* and *King Coffin* are not only statements of the writer's inner agony but are as Mary Martin Rountree puts it, "portraits of the artist as a middle-aged failure." Yet out of an apocalyptic awareness of his own growing psychic disintegration, which culminated in a suicide attempt in 1932, there grew in the poet, quite slowly at first, a sense of hope and personal triumph. What made the difference, what allowed Aiken to emerge at last from the inner hell that his best fiction records, is, in Rountree's words, his "buoyant affirmation of his belief in the ultimate value of his life's work as a 'priest of consciousness.'"[2]

In finding again his vocation, after temporarily losing sight of it in the late twenties, Aiken accepted his own suffering and that of the new decade of the thirties, both being intertwined, and turned it into apocalyptic visions

---

[1] Ibid., 115.
[2] Mary Martin Rountree, "Conrad Aiken's Heroes: Portraits of the Artist as a Middle-Aged Failure," *Studies in the Literary Imagination* XIII, 2 (Fall 1980), 82.

of the future that pointed to both personal and social rebirth. The role of the pilgrim that he had accepted in his best poetry after 1917 was only temporarily forgotten in the poet's fictional plunges into his psychic pain and in the continuing agony of divorce and personal struggle with his second wife. The recovering of that role prepared him for his deepest visions and at last initiated him into that loose-knit society of modern writers who became not so much priests but shamans who could bring back from ordeals of personal agony their visions of hope and cosmic harmony. As Rountree puts it, *Ushant* is "far more concerned with finding an inner peace and harmony than with building a reputation as a man of letters."[3] But for the apocalyptic poet like Aiken peace and harmony can only be had from visions that spring from profound encounters with chaos. As early as 1931 Houston Peterson was presenting in his book-length study of Aiken this essential theme in the poet's work of a musical harmony that can be perceived only by plunging into chaos.

As I have earlier suggested, Aiken's plunge into his second marriage was unconsciously an attempt to relive again the kind of chaos that had destroyed his parents. Thus like his father he would seek in a hundred devious and obvious ways to destroy Clarissa Lorenz and then kill himself. But as a pilgrim he would also cling to his continuing belief that chaos must be encountered and that it can be overcome if the pilgrim maintains that faith in a divine harmony that he learned from Santayana, his chief philosophical mentor. Clarissa Lorenz would end her memoir by comparing Hemingway and Aiken as men who suffered through several marriages, ravaging their partners and others in their demonic quest for artistic accomplishment. Yet Hemingway, because he could at last see himself only in terms of such images as those of famous writer, great literary artist, renowned sportsman, and sexual athlete, suffered slow psychic decay and a final mental depression and suicide. Aiken in fact was moving in 1931 into the kind of depression that leads to suicide. The poet, however, as he had predicted in *Changing Mind,* the pivotal poem that links *The Divine Pilgrim* with the Preludes, would overcome the controlling power of Narcissus in order to encounter both his own inner creative powers and that love that would make his third marriage extremely fruitful and that would renew his friendship with Eliot and other literary comrades.

Aiken's plunge into chaos as a pilgrim rather than as simply a recorder of his own miseries begins with his composition of the first Preludes in the

---

[3]Ibid., 84.

late twenties and continues into the early 1930s with his one expressionistic drama, *The Coming Forth by Day of Osiris Jones*, and with the first drafts of *Ushant* as well as with the novels *Great Circle* and *King Coffin*. These works record Aiken's movement through both personal and social chaos, and by the thirties he could see himself as a representative man, one who must suffer both his own and world civilization's apocalyptic collapse and rebirth in World War II. But even as we see Aiken the representative man emerging in the thirties to become the central figure in *Ushant*, we must keep in mind that Aiken is really several people, and one of them is always the artist as ravager described by Lorenz in one of the frankest literary memoirs of the century. "What ordinary mortals can't swallow about artists," Lorenz writes, "is the ravaging of others. But the daemon will continue to destroy with impunity. Art, after all, is born of a colossal ego re-creating the world in its image."[4] In *King Coffin* and *Great Circle* Aiken revealed, as he had done in the Symphonies, his enormous narcissism and its attendant possessiveness and ravaging of others, accompanied by self-hatred and destructiveness of an extremely lethal nature. In *Great Circle* Andy Cather suddenly sees that he has been destroying his own wife (in reality, Aiken's Jessie, the first wife) and himself: "You are deliberately seeking a catastrophe--you are yourself in the act of creating a disaster."[5] When he sees the police investigating a suicide in the river, Cather cries out desperately to himself, as Aiken surely must have done many times: "Cling to life, you poor bastard."[6]

Psychoanalysts have clearly established that the offspring of a suicidal parent is often haunted by impulses of self-destruction. For instance, Walker Percy, whose father killed himself, amply reveals in several novels the haunted feeling that children of suicidal parents have. But the self-hating, self-destructive narcissist also can many times see himself as a god who has the right to manipulate and even destroy others. Aiken deals with this aspect of himself in *King Coffin*, where the protagonist feels powerful and significant enough to ravage anyone he chooses; and yet he sees that his desire to destroy an innocent victim is a projection of his own self-destructiveness and self-hatred. Jasper Ammen, the author tells us, "has self-destruction as his aim from the outset."[7] The daemon that ravages others

---

[4]Clarissa M. Lorenz, *Lorelei Two* (Athens: The University of Georgia Press, 1983), 220.

[5]Conrad Aiken, *Great Circle* (New York: Charles Scribner, 1933), 8.

[6]Ibid., 38.

[7]Conrad Aiken, "Author's Preface," *3 Novels* (New York: McGraw-Hill, 1965), 12.

is also the daemon that destroys the ravager unless that power can be exorcized. Lorenz is thus incorrect in saying that Aiken's daemon "will continue to destroy with impunity." The daemon, unless checked, will destroy the psyche within which it lives. Although Aiken did not ever banish this shadow side of himself, he did bring it under control and even made it play a part in the creative process, which consists of several forces and not simply the ravaging power that Lorenz and others have equated with the artistic process. Within the psyche, Aiken's pilgrimage revealed, is also the power of love, which was gradually released as he overcame the power of the ravaging shadow. If there had not been a love flow in his life, Aiken would have gone the way of his friend John Gould Fletcher into insanity and suicide or the way of his friend Malcolm Lowry into alcoholism. These were well known ways of destruction for many depressed writers of the twentieth century.

In 1932, the year of his suicide attempt and the lowest point of depression in his entire life, Aiken was reaching out to help Fletcher, who himself had become deranged and had attempted suicide. Fletcher was, with Aiken's help, committed to London's Bethlehem Hospital. Aiken's loving concern for both Fletcher and Malcolm Lowry reveals that he was not under the total control of the ravaging monster of art that Lorenz would largely experience. That she saw mainly this aspect of Aiken and not the other sides of him she finally admits at the end of her memoir:

> Decades after we broke up I started reading his works and tributes, reminders winnowed out of my consciousness. I began to see what he was all about--his aspirations, motives, commitments, and the poet's dilemmas. Much of what he wrote came out of our relationship, but I wasn't ready to grasp it earlier. Now I feel a sense of discovery; many of his poems are illuminated by this latent understanding.[8]

What Lorenz, as well as Aiken himself, could not understand in the crisis years of the early thirties was that at last Aiken was coming to grips with the deepest aspects of himself, both the creative and the destructive powers he carried within his psyche. Complete disintegration was possible, and he accepted this ultimate challenge of his life. The details of personal disintegration can be read in both his work and his life as we see it reported

---

[8]Lorenz, 221-222.

by Lorenz. But the works of the early thirties also suggest that Aiken was accepting the challenge of the Great Depression and the rise of totalitarianism. Prophetically, he saw that humanity would once again encounter an apocalyptic destructiveness, to be followed, as Aiken would tell us in the Preludes and other works, by an overcoming of the shadow forces. Probably the most neglected important poem of Aiken's canon, "The Poet in Granada," which grew out of Aiken's visit to Spain in 1931 with Lowry and Lorenz, prophesies the coming destructive war in that country as a harbinger of even greater, worldwide destruction. Yet it ends with a celebration of the everlasting beauty of nature, unspoiled by hatred and fear, a symbol for Aiken of the harmony that undergirds the world even in the midst of human destruction. Written about the sacrificial death of the archetypal poet who plays the role of Christ as he dies and is resurrected, the poem fittingly is dedicated to modern Spain's greatest poet, Federico García Lorca, who would himself be executed by the fascists in the kind of sacrificial death that Aiken in the poem predicted for the many poets, artists, and philosophers who in fact in the thirties were falling victim to totalitarian violence. Thus Aiken in the poem wonders if he must die also, concluding that he is ready to be sacrificed, if necessary, as a priest of consciousness.

The growing agonies of the Great Depression in America and Europe after 1930, along with the dangerous political climate, called forth more than ever in Aiken's mind the role of a priest of consciousness. Like Emerson, he saw himself as the poet playing the role of representative man, one who, like the primitive shaman, bears the burdens of humanity and through his suffering brings forth new visions of the renewal of humanity. Thus the agony of both personal and social disintegration forced Aiken as representative man to seek the deepest creative powers within himself. As the awareness of approaching war grew stronger, many began to believe that civilization itself would be destroyed in the conflagration. Yeats in poems like "Lapis Lazuli" and Eliot in "Burnt Norton" and "East Coker" were recording similar feelings of apocalyptic destruction with possible world renewal to follow. But more than either one of these poets, Aiken even as early as 1930 was experiencing small visions of both personal and social renewal. In his one expressionistic drama, *The Coming Forth by Day of Osiris Jones*, the poet records, even as he moves toward a nearly successful suicide attempt, his belief that the chaos experienced by everyone would work for the good of all. Probably the most significant line in the play is "Chaos--hurray!--has come again," because for the shamanistic poet like Aiken, the opportunity has again come for the artist-philosopher once more to demonstrate that it is possible to accept in one's soul that chaos that threatens death . Further, by accepting it, the poet shows others that it is possible to overcome psychic chaos and, by doing so, affirm and release the creative powers within the soul. This line also refers directly to the play's theme that only within a period of apocalyptic chaos can the divine element, symbolized by Osiris, fully emerge and become the center of human existence. James Joyce, Richard Ellmann writes, discovered the play's title and from it alone saw that Aiken was writing about the same subject he was dealing with in *Finnegans Wake*. Joyce in *Finnegans Wake* depicts the death of the common man, Finnegan, in the age of chaos that was succeeding the dying of the Viconian age of the democracies. From his death would arise once more the cyclic process Vico describes in *The New Science*, the heroic man Finn. Aiken in his reading of the archaeological studies of Flinders Petrie and of the *Egyptian Book of the Dead* had come up with essentially the same ideas Joyce found in Vico. Like Joyce, he applied these ideas to the modern scene. Unlike Aiken, Joyce while proclaiming the apocalypse of the new heroic man and of a renewed civilization was sinking into a deepening depression from which he would never emerge until his death only two years after the publication of *Finnegans Wake*.

Aiken of necessity had tied his own personal development to his apocalyptic writing. Even as he sank after 1930 into personal depression, he also was being delivered, through his writing and his struggle to live, from his personal demons. In *Great Circle*, also being written during his years of greatest depression and published in 1933, he records, as the novel ends, the fierce personal psychoanalysis he put himself through in this novel. Thus the protagonist Andy Cather cries out, "You in the flesh again, redivivus." Cather at last begins to see what the beginning process of psychic exorcism really means:

> It would be good to touch, for the last time, that agony, and to exorcise it . . . the strange and exciting mixture of astonishment and suffering with which--at a moment of discovery--one loses oneself in order to create oneself. The end is still conscious of its beginnings. Birth that remembers death.[9]

The novel ends with the theme of *Osiris Jones*, summed up in the concept of Great Circle, which is that an individual even in his dying can return

---

[9]*Great Circle*, 303.

through proper recollection to the time of his birth and see those moments of transcendent glory that Romantics like Wordsworth and Shelley, two poets often in Aiken's mind, always point to as the anchor of the human soul. The experience of rebirth described in *Great Circle* would always remain at the forefront of the poet's attention; and at the end of *Ushant* he would have turned this personal vision into a vision of worldwide apocalyptic renewal. The great vision at the end of *Ushant* states Aiken's experience during his early and middle thirties of at once seeming to drown in despondency and strong suicidal impulses and at the same time of seeming to rise through a series of imaginative insights to a sustaining harmony, borne by the wings of music:

> Yes, now we are drowning--all of us are drowning, but as we drown, we seem somehow to be floating upward, we are all floating upward and singing. Floating upward towards that vast, that outspread, sheet of illuminated music, which is the world (*Ushant,* 365).

This personal experience, Aiken often suggests in *Ushant,* is linked with the social upheavals of the thirties and forties when war seemed to threaten to blot out civilization.

Ushant is written from the perspective of a man who has survived both the Great Depression and World War II, and in that brief period before the Russians announced their possession of the nuclear bomb and before America's deep involvement in Korea, Aiken draws both a personal and a collective sigh of relief and even experiences a kind of joyful and sentimental reflection. Thus Steven E. Olson calls *Ushant* "sentimentally celebratory," and indeed it is. After all, Aiken calls his *Ushant* an essay, which suggests that this book is not so much a record of his life as a poetic statement about himself, his friends, and his times. As such, *Ushant,* which continues the record of Demarest's career in *Blue Voyage* (D. stands for Demarest, who is a persona of Aiken's), is many faceted, playful, even joyful in announcing the fact that Demarest-Aiken has found a meaningful place in life, has not, that is, succumbed to his inner demons. But the joyful sections of the book--and Aiken, speaking of Lowry, asks why indeed genius cannot be at times joyful--only cover up, as works in the symbolist tradition often do, the book's central theme, which is the individual's quest for greater consciousness. The deepest significance of this major concluding vision is contained in its concluding description. Beyond the sight of the "sheet of illuminated music" Aiken sees the "Teacher of the West," that Christ-like, saving figure who emerges fitfully within the soul. But first, he says, it is only a hand of the teacher that the "we"--and this "we" is all important--can glimpse. The figure seems to "sing to someone else." Then the narrator becomes aware that "we rise, we rise, ourselves now like notes of music arranging themselves in a divine harmony, a divine unison, which, as it had no beginning, can have no end--" (*Ushant*, 365). Thus at first the "we"--Aiken's comrades and by extension all other priests of consciousness--seem to be lost, cut off from the divine teacher; but suddenly there is the awareness of a "rising" to encounter both divine harmony and the Teacher of the West. The meaning of this most important of Aiken's visions in *Ushant* can only be grasped if it is seen in relationship to the teachings of the poet's three masters, Santayana, Freud, and Potter.

I will examine the philosophical influence of Santayana, the psychological influence of Freud, and the religious influence of Potter--and how those influences manifest themselves in Aiken's life and work--in the concluding chapters on the poet's philosophical, psychological, and religious views. But in summary, Aiken received from Santayana the teaching of a divine harmony that must be apprehended for the individual to achieve an expanded consciousness and with it an increasing flow of love. The action that leads to expansion of consciousness is contemplation. Thus Santayana sums up his "A Brief History of My Opinions": "And it is only in contemplative moments that life is truly vital, when routine gives place to intuition, and experience is synthesized and brought before the spirit in its sweep and truth." Only through contemplation can there be a truly creative emotional flow that was so important to all the Romantics. Thus Santayana continues: "The intention of my philosophy has certainly been to attain, if possible, such wide intuitions, and to celebrate the emotions with which they fill the mind."[10] From Freud Aiken took the idea that through dreams, as well as through "intuitions" gained by Santayana's contemplation, the pilgrim could receive insights into both his creative powers and into his dark side that had to be faced in order for the individual to achieve expanded consciousness. From Freud and from Potter, as well as from both the Transcendentalists and the symbolists, he came to accept the idea of comrades working together to expand human consciousness. Far more than Santayana, Aiken was aware of the alienation and destructiveness of the modern age, but *Ushant* indicates, not always clearly due to Aiken's

---

[10]*The Philosophy of Santayana*, ed. Irwin Edman (New York: The Modern Library, 1936), 21.

stream-of-consciousness method, that through the emergence of new visionary power humankind would pass through an apocalyptic age to emerge into the new age that Grandfather Potter had preached as a rebel Unitarian. Thus Aiken sees humanity itself reaching for visionary experience that would usher in this new age: ". . . as now, and always, all mankind were soldiers; all of them engaged in the endless and desperate war on the unconscious" (*Ushant*, 362).

The concept of apocalypse traditionally refers both to the destructiveness that ends one age and the visions that make possible and sustain a new age containing wider consciousness and deeper emotional power than was to be found at the end of the previous age. *Ushant* contains a series of personal visions scattered among Aiken's often deeply felt recording of the events of his life that prepare the reader for the culminating vision of comrades drowning and yet at the same time rising to encounter divine harmony and the divine Teacher. The metaphor of drowning is one of Aiken's many metaphors for the growing destructiveness of the dying age. For Aiken the primary forms that destructiveness took were two: the narcissism that breeds the demons he had experienced in his own soul as well as the totalitarian repression that seeks to imprison individuals in a collective and dark unconsciousness by denying them the time and the means to achieve the dreams and intuitions necessary to increase consciousness. For Aiken the true barbarian is he who denies the role of vision in activating the soul. The barbarian acts only from unconscious urges and drives that control his existence or from the state-supported propaganda that manipulates both conscious and unconscious aspects of the mind.

Politics for Aiken was only a surface manifestation of humanity's movement toward self-transcendence. Although he played a small role in supporting Hubert Humphrey for president in 1968, Aiken's larger political viewpoint, as expressed in *Ushant*, was "slightly Olympian" (U, 351). He confessed to having "once voted for Debs" but goes on to say that "he had never found it possible to take more than a casual and superficial interest in practical politics, viewing it, as he did, as inevitably a passing phase, and probably a pretty primitive one, and something, again, that the evolution of consciousness would in its own season take care of" (U, 351). Only in the continuing growth of consciousness could humanity pass through the revolutionary upheavals of the twentieth century in order to find that new human development that Aiken and the nineteenth-century Transcendentalists before him, his grandfather most of all, had been forecasting. But political revolution in itself was not a movement toward larger consciousness but only the birthpangs of that movement: "Revolutions were a waste both of time and human material;--you lost a hundred or more years only to find yourself just where you'd begun" (U, 351). Thus for Aiken modern revolutions brought forth the imprisoning of humanity's deepest creative powers: "A revolution was an attempt to freeze society on a particular level, and this was itself stultifying, no matter what that level might be" (*Ushant*, 351).

Aiken in one sense agreed with Robert Frost's idea that the only real revolution was the one-person revolution. Aiken's individualism was in its own way as intense as Frost's, and yet this individualism, linked partly to the historical figure of William Blackstone, was based essentially on small groups of friends who were loosely connected with all others, largely unknown still, who were moving through an apocalyptic century toward an age of enlarged consciousness. In *Ushant* Aiken is established in the perceived role of artist-servant-hero that he had been discovering in the twenties and had first enunciated in *Blue Voyage*. To discover this role of artist-servant-hero meant a withdrawal from others and a plunge into the psyche to discover both unrealized destructive and creative powers. But the journey itself of the artist-servant-hero, who is essentially everyone moving as a pilgrim on the road to higher consciousness, is made in the company of others. Thus the most important vision in *Ushant* is that of the Teacher of the West who instructs not only Aiken but his friend Lowry and their feminine companions--two men and two women whose journey stood for that of all groups that move slowly, usually ignored and misunderstood, toward a new age. Ushant is a symbol of both the forces that impede and threaten the pilgrim, but it is also a symbol of that "world so overflowing with beauty, strangeness, doubt, terror, and divinity," described in the words of the Nietzsche epigraph to *Ushant*. Thus Aiken ends his autobiographical essay with his greatest vision of the Teacher of the West. He ends it with his vision of both drowning and coming into new life in the "divine unison" because, as the Nietzsche epigraph tells us, once the new world has been glimpsed we can never "be content with the *man of the present day*." And like Nietzsche who speaks of "our conscience and consciousness full of such burning desire," Aiken speaks of *we* and never of the *I*, that lonely Transcendentalist like Thoreau at Walden pond. In fact, Aiken's vision of Ushant is but one vision of a paradise that his own daughter had written of in her poem "The Playlanders." As Jean ended her poem with a "dream-song," so Aiken ends his prose-poem *Ushant* with his own dream-song of both personal and collective renewal through vision leading to an education by a divine Teacher who points toward a "divine harmony" we all rise to.

For those who read *Ushant* mainly for its literary reminiscences--and it is extremely valuable for these alone--there is often the surprise of how celebratory (and even sentimental, as Olson has suggested) the work is. Aiken uses the term "abundance and joy" to speak of those moments of creative wonder that he experienced in composing his work, in his own dreams and intuitions, and in his work with Eliot, Pound, Lowry, and other geniuses of his day. He even defends Lowry's moments of joy against those who believe the modern writer must wallow in sadness. Why shouldn't the genius enjoy himself?, he asks. At the same time he reveals the envy and rage that pervaded a brilliant London literary life. Describing Katherine Mansfield and Virginia Woolf as they "measured each other with a locked gaze of feral enmity," he can only sum up the London literary world for Lowry as "a jungle scene, simply this literary forest" (U, 292-293). Of his own struggles with the alcoholic Lowry, he records an even greater pain than he knew with Eliot, his other literary brother. But with Lowry, or Hambo as he calls him, Aiken could experience the joy of genius:

> [F]or surely of all the literary folk whom D. had ever encountered, there had been none among them who had been so visibly or happily alight with genius--not that the Tsetse hadn't manifested something of the same thing, to be sure--controlling it moreover to better purpose; but in Hambo it had been more moving and convincing, and alive, for its very *un*controlledness, its spontaneity and gay recklessness, not to mention its infectiously gleeful delight in itself. And why . . . shouldn't genius damned well enjoy itself? (*Ushant*, 292)

The joy that Aiken could experience at times with both Eliot and Lowry was based on a love that had survived bitter struggle between himself and the other two, so different from each other. What *Ushant* does not speak of in any detail is how Aiken moved from his own bitterness and depression of 1932 to a discovery of new wellsprings of joy and love. Instead he devoted his most important series of poems, the Preludes, to this subject.

The Preludes can and should be read in connection with *Ushant* and the major fiction of the twenties and thirties. But no other work so brilliantly displays Aiken's descent into his own psyche in search of a renewal of creative energy. I have already suggested that *Changing Mind* was the real beginning of the Preludes because in this work Aiken announced his discovery of the way of suffering which led past Narcissus to the inner powers of both creativity and destruction.

In the Preludes the pilgrim moves thus into the center of chaos and death, absorbs the stress of both by affirming unity, and thus finds new love and vision. In the first group of Preludes, called *Preludes for Memnon*, the poet states the condition of modern man, caught up as he is in despair and pain and held in the grip of possessing images. But he also states his belief in the keys of vision, knowledge, and love. In the second set of Preludes, *Time in the Rock*, he defines basic metaphysical attitudes not in abstractions--though his language is sometimes mathematical and scientific--but in the responses of the individual on a mythic journey. In the Preludes the idealism of the Symphonies is maintained and the vision of humankind's corruption is expanded and deepened. Nowhere in Aiken's work is there so deep an affirmation of the unifying power that links the rock and the bloodstream. But, as Frederick J. Hoffman has pointed out, an idealism that does not face pain and death is both dangerous and meaningless. In the Preludes Aiken has subjected all of his beliefs to the test of pain. By doing so he demonstrates that man can live continually with pain and the threat of death when he affirms his own creative powers in the midst of destructiveness.

The Preludes are Aiken's great poems of pilgrimage. *Preludes for Memnon* takes the reader with the pilgrim into the poet's soul, where one hears ". . . the uprush of angelic wings, the beating/ Of wings demonic, from the abyss of the mind:" (CP, 499). The abyss of the mind is, of course, the unconscious, but Aiken on his journey must go deeper than Freud went: he must affirm the meaning of man's mind in both its angelic and its demonic guises. But he must also begin where Freud began: with the sickness of the soul. Aiken's definition of this sickness is both Jungian and Freudian. Thus he summons the archetype of the anima as well as the archetype of the shadow. The shadow makes its appearance in the form of chaos threatening to overwhelm the pilgrim, or else it comes as a voice that denies all, as the image of the great nothingness: "Ice: silence: death: the abyss of Nothing" (CP, 501). With the apprehension of nothingness comes the bad dreams, the destructive nightmares, visions of soul sickness: "O God, O God, let the sore soul have peace./ Deliver it from this bondage of harsh dreams" (CP, 501).

The pilgrim's response to the challenge of the shadow must be to plunge ever deeper into the hidden depths: "Let the fleet soul go nimbly,--/ Down,--Down,--down,--from step to step of dark,--" (CP, 502). The plunge into the chaos hidden in the soul, the uncovering, that is, of the hidden feelings of despair lurking in the unconscious, brings man to an icy nothingness; but the reward for the plunger who affirms unity is love: "Love, be that glory and that sense of brightness./ You are what chaos yielded. Be my star" (CP, 520). Affirmation of unity plus the stress of meeting the inner shadow yields love; love itself, along with the renewed vision of unity, becomes the guide, or star, for the voyaging soul on its way to greater vision and deeper creativity. For a long time the soul does not know its destination, but as clarity grows with vision in the second set of Preludes, *Time in the Rock*, the poet sees his destination: "And it is you: toward the light you move/ as silently, as gravely, as a ship/ counters the evening tide:" (CP, 755). The way past chaos and pain encountered on the journey, the way past the evening tide of a dying civilization, is through the growth of the light of the spirit that guides man beyond darkness to the banquet of creativity.

Having absorbed the wisdom of Emerson and Melville, Aiken sees nature as both destroyer and preserver, both enemy and teacher. "The maelstrom has us all," he says in *Preludes to Memnon*, but later in the same work he can say, "Keep in the heart the journal nature keeps" (CP, 520, 547). For Aiken, nature and man are indissolubly linked, yet both are but outward manifestations of deeper currents of energy welling up from the unconscious mind and working in the profound, daily miracles of the atoms.

The horror of the maelstrom is necessary for the refinement of the heart. This refinement makes possible the deepening unity between the blood and the rock, the self and the Self:

> Yes, and you have noted
> how then the chemistry of the soul at midnight
> secretes peculiar virtue from such poisons:
> you have been pleased: rubbed metaphoric hands:
> saying to yourself that the suffering, the shame,
> the pity, and the self-pity, and the horror,
> that all these things refine love's angel,
> filth in flame made perfect. (CP, 736)

Time in the Rock thus defines the essential and continuing pilgrimage. In the midst of an ordinary day the pilgrim seeks the guidance not only of love and of the powers of nature but also of the voices of the wise old ancestors of man: "What did we read last night about Confucius/ what was my dream of Anna Livia" (CP, 750). Virgil and Dante also guide him but the times are not now so simple as they once were, he says. Finally it is with the complete acceptance of all--both the wisdom of sages and the simplicity of nature--that Aiken ends *Time in the Rock*:

> Simple one, simpleton,
> when will you learn the flower's simplicity--
> lie open to all comers, permit yourself
> to be rifled--fruitfully too--by other selves?
> Self, and other self--permit them, permit them-- (CP, 757)

Like Eliot at the end of *East Coker* Aiken urges man to an acceptance of everything and to a pushing on into the dark waters for a deeper communion. For Eliot and Aiken both the descent into the dark mind of self is a descent into Self, or God, even as the way out of self into the world leads one back into Self. Thus, in the words of one of the epigraphs of Eliot's *Four Quartets*, the way up and the way down are one and the same. In *Preludes for Memnon* Aiken defines the essential relationship between self and Self: "Search the dark kingdom. It is to self you come,--/ And that is God. It is the seed of seeds" (CP, 515). Thus Aiken can say with the *Upanishads:* "Atman is Brahman and Brahman is all." Yet for the mythic quester the philosophical statement is not an end in itself but only a talisman that aids the quester as he passes in and out of unconscious mind to encounter the divine Self.

To encounter the Self is to know, Aiken tells us, the source of expanding consciousness; to serve the Self is at once to suffer and to encounter again and again those moments of vision that constitute the ever-evolving consciousness through which the human race will move to a higher level than any it has previously known. In the Preludes' vision of Self we find Aiken's most deeply Romantic viewpoint. Emerson had posited soul and oversoul as the divine basis of human existence. Plunging more deeply into Hinduism and Buddhism than Emerson ever did, Aiken establishes the Self as at once both the divine center of man and the one God of the universe. Yet Aiken could never rest with the kind of tranquillity induced through meditation by the Buddhists of both East and West. Aiken was too much the modern man to adopt a pose of relaxed certainty. For him to be modern meant to be haunted by inner suffering and the outer pressures of an apocalyptic age. As poet and writer of fiction, Aiken is at his best when he is under the pressure of outer and inner terrors. To be an artist--literary or otherwise--was for Aiken the supreme task of the modern man seeking higher consciousness. Furthermore, Aiken as a poet with one foot in the symbolist camp inevitably had to plunge many times into complexities of thought while at the same time seeking the meaning of artistic form as a way of preserving himself from the confusions of both the mind and the dissident and destructive age in which he lived. For Hoffman and R. P. Blackmur the concern with form is central to the Preludes. Thus Blackmur writes that the Preludes "present the actual predicaments of the enacting consciousness with the minimum resort to formula and the maximum approach to form."[11] Hoffman sees Aiken's selection of Memnon as the central image of the first set of Preludes because it deals with Aiken's main problem, overcoming time through form. Thus "poetic form is an act of constantly remaking. Forms are not enduring; even the colossus of Memnon has been cracked by earthquake."[12]

Blackmur and Hoffman, both formalists, cannot see beyond Aiken's modernist concern with time and consciousness, seen by them as conscious awareness and the need somehow to overcome time and its ravages. Hoffman, of course, is aware of the pilgrim nature of Aiken's poetic movement in time and rightly sees that to survive at all he must overcome the shoutings of chaos within his soul and the souls of others that threaten him, shoutings that ultimately spring from a sense of nothingness that too deep an awareness of time's triumph over life can instill in the individual. For Hoffman, always subtle in his analysis of the modernist element in Aiken, believes that "mastery of chaos comes from a creative knowing."[13] Yet Hoffman never defines how this creative knowing masters chaos. Instead one may say, after examining the deconstructionist aspects of the Preludes, that it is through knowing that Aiken overcomes the mind's dependence on abstractions and on form itself in order to plunge into the Self within everything. But the concept of the encounter with Self is too Romantic an idea for Hoffman to deal with, though he is aware, without using the term, of Aiken's deconstructionist stance.

Hoffman thus points out that *Preludes for Memnon* ends with the theme of the destruction of old god figures. Having begun this first set of Preludes with the image of winter--"Winter for a moment takes the mind"--Aiken must plunge on into the mind's snows, its slippery paths,/ Walls bayonetted with ice, leaves ice-encased" (CP, 498). Yet throughout these poems, as I have already indicated, he reveals visionary glimpses of that divine element he has been seeking within himself since "Tetélestai" in 1917, the element that for him alone can overcome chaos and make artistic form, no matter

---

[11]Quoted by Hoffman, *Conrad Aiken*, 127.
[12]Ibid., 122.
[13]Ibid., 126.

how brief, possible within time's context. But artistic form alone--as it is for Wallace Stevens, whom Blackmur and Hoffman compare with Aiken--cannot be the highest goal of the pilgrim. Expanded consciousness for all who desire it is that goal, as it was the goal for major Romantics from Blake and Wordsworth to Emerson and Whitman.

That *Preludes for Memnon* is not the peak of Aiken's poetic vision can be seen in the way he introduces in LVI his best known image of deconstruction, that of Verlaine proclaiming the need to wring the neck of rhetoric and then to wipe out godhead. From there Aiken moves on to a quiet ending of the series of poems that admit that "No language leaps this chasm like a lightning:/ Here is no message of assuagement. . ." (CP, 573). Messages for Aiken were as hollow as both rhetoric and godhead because they had become centered in abstract thinking, had become logocentric and thus detached from love. It remains for the ninety-six poems of *Preludes to Definition,* called *Time in the Rock,* which Hoffman says is "undoubtedly his greatest work," to present Aiken's final deconstruction of the forms of both rhetoric and religion so that he can rediscover the Self in terms of love, joy, and abundance. Thus he proclaims the mysticism of no-words: "Mysticism, but let us have no words,/ angels, but let us have no fantasies,/ churches, but let us have no creeds,/ no dead gods hung on crosses in a shop,/ nor beads nor prayers nor faith nor sin nor penance:/ and yet, let us believe, let us believe (CP, 674)." In denouncing creeds Aiken takes his stance with Emerson and Whitman. Following them and the doctrine of correspondences, Aiken gives us the flower as the tangible statement of God: "Mysticism, but let it be a flower,/ let it be the hand that reaches for the flower. . ." (CP, 674). From this beginning Aiken moves boldly to assert "the horror,/ that all these things refine love's angel, filth in flame made perfect" (CP, 736). Finally in the last Prelude he can assert the triumph of summer over winter and the primacy of the Self in all things: "Self, and other self--permit them, permit them--it is summer still, winter can do no more" (CP, 757).

Fittingly *Time in the Rock* appeared in 1936, the year of the greatest sense of personal renewal Aiken probably ever knew. That year he revisited Savannah for the first time since 1901 and experienced, as *Ushant* tells us, a sense of new life. At last he was overcoming the threatening urges of suicide. The same year he met Mary Hoover, who would become his third wife, and in Boston of that year with Mary and the painter Edward Burra he experienced more deeply than ever before the two great loves he describes in *Ushant, eros* and *caritas.* The old, destructive relationship with Clarissa Lorenz was at last put behind him; and in 1937, when Lorenz refused to grant him a divorce, Aiken with Burra and Mary went to Mexico to seek there a quick divorce. That year at Cuernavaca Mary and Conrad were involved in some of the momentous events with Lowry that went into the latter's novel *Under the Volcano.* Aiken himself is a major character in this novel that is probably the greatest fictional statement about alcoholism to be found in English. By 1938 Conrad installed Mary as the third wife of Jeake's House in Rye and launched a new and happy chapter in his literary life. Only the coming of the long feared holocaust that was the second World War would catapult them from the beloved Rye to an America Aiken thought he had left behind him.

Aiken's renewal as a man was intimately connected with his work on the Preludes and *Ushant,* not to mention lesser poetry, fiction and critical essays. For Mary he wrote a series of sonnets, *And in the Human Heart,* which were linked with *Time in the Rock.* Aiken's literary work was not interrupted by the war, but except for *Brownstone Ecologues,* there was not the intensity to be found in the Preludes. Except for several philosophical poems after World War II Aiken's major work after 1940 would be *Ushant,* one of the great autobiographies of American literature.

Brownstone Ecologues and Other Poems, which appeared in 1942, contains some excellent religious verse that grew out of the spiritual struggles of the thirties. Aiken's awareness of Christ and similar redemptive figures emerges whenever Aiken felt his own life threatened by crisis. Experiencing as he did the agony of the Allies fighting the temporarily victorious Axis powers in the years between 1940 and 1942, a time when civilization itself might have fallen to the barbarians, Aiken records the pressures of wartime life in America. Since this volume is one of his works of that religious renewal that he experienced after he entered the last phase of his life as a permanent resident in America, I will reserve discussion of it in a chapter on Aiken's religious views. But what above all both this volume and the Preludes reveal is that he had achieved renewed poetic powers through suffering and a continuing belief in cosmic harmony. Having rejected Eliot's turning to medievalism in poems like *Ash-Wednesday,* Aiken resolutely accepted a poetry based on his philosophical meditations and on a pan-mythic view of humanity's quest for the divine ground. Aiken's personal reconciliation with Eliot in the late thirties was paralleled by his discovery with the publication of *Four Quartets* that Eliot too had adopted both a philosophical and comparative mythological view as the basis for his last great poetic effort.

In 1965 Aiken described to me at length how much he admired the *Quartets*, though he had reservations about "Burnt Norton." But like Eliot himself he believed that each succeeding quartet was better than the one before it. My own analysis in an article discussing the archetypal symbolism of the Preludes and the *Quartets* reveals the striking similarity between the imagery and the philosophy contained within the major work of the two poets. Once again as at Harvard and in the twenties when Eliot was borrowing from the Symphonies to write *The Waste Land* the two poets were revealing in their work a deep sympathy neither one probably ever fully understood. What they had most in common during the late thirties and the decade of the forties--the period of much of their best work--is a sense of their own continuing pilgrimage in quest of deeper emotional relationships and a profounder awareness of the metaphysical realm of existence.

Much literary criticism since World War II has seen significant poets in the symbolist tradition like Stevens, Eliot, Aiken, and Yeats as figures who seek creativity and order through the exercise of the imagination. Discussing Aiken's poem "Overture to Today" Hoffman speaks of an "emphasis upon human creativity" that "makes a perfect Aiken-Stevens sense" and then goes to say that for Aiken and Stevens "The creative mode is the imagination, the 'world becoming word.'"[14] Hoffman is correct concerning the role of imagination and the word, but he is incorrect to say that "the paradoxes of time and eternity" were not real for Aiken, as they were for Eliot. Hoffman is also wrong in referring to Aiken's philosophy as "'romantic naturalism,'" a viewpoint the poet rejected after his first volume, *Earth Triumphant,* in favor of what he would in time call the viewpoint of the divine pilgrim. *Divine* in this case suggests a "sacred" or metaphysical realm of existence referred to in some philosophies as eternity, or Being. Aiken's return to Santayana after a brief period of being a Nietzschean "naturalist" meant the acceptance of the divine element in life. The Romantic side of Nietzsche, which was the philosopher's dominant side, accepted a world ruled by the god Dionysus. Nietzsche's chief modern disciple, Heidegger, began his work with the concept of Being and later in his exploration of language used the concept of the gods, thus reminding one of Santayana, who said that the "height of poetry is to speak the language of the gods."[15] That Hoffman is wrong in assuming that Aiken remained a "romantic naturalist" is seen in the critic's conclusion that Aiken's viewpoint leads him "to *accept* [Hoffman's

---

[14]Hoffman, 152.
[15]George Santayana, *Three Philosophical Poets* (Garden City, New York, 1953), 21.

italics] the paradoxical isolation that is his lot."[16] Instead of accepting isolation as his lot, Aiken early realized that he must find a way *out* of isolation or else go mad or become so depressed that he would have to kill himself. The role of the divine pilgrim then is to discover, through making brief contacts with the metaphysical realm, a way of successfully relating to other people. Aiken as writer and young philosopher first adopted a kind of romantic naturalism and then, with "Tetélestai," he took up the style of symbolism and with it a Romantic awareness of a metaphysical realm that is to be found in some symbolists and not in others.

The problem of the relationship of the modern poet to an inherited Romantic metaphysics and religion is one of the great neglected problems of modern literary history. In the three chapters that follow I will deal with it in terms of Aiken's philosophy, psychology, and religion. To do so I will use both internal evidence within the work and biographical evidence, including my own discussions with Aiken. Like two other poets who were both symbolists and Romantics--Eliot and Yeats--Aiken remained true to both traditions and even at times wrote in terms of a symbolist-naturalist tradition that seems to deny all metaphysical reality. Yet the divine pilgrim is still the central concept of his life and work. James Lovic Allen has denominated certain critics as "humanistic imaginationists" (Ellmann and Harold Bloom chief among them) in that they seek to show that Yeats, for instance, did not actually believe in the myths or the spirits he writes about. I agree with Allen--and I think the evidence is there to prove it--that Yeats is in part an old-fashioned Romantic who did believe in myth and spirit as much as did Wordsworth, Shelley, and Blake. An unstructured mysticism was chiefly what Romanticism after 1790 consisted of, that and the concomitant quest for the creative emotions of love and joy. And I would apply what Allen writes about Yeats on this matter equally to Aiken and even to a certain extent to Eliot:

> These points educe the fact that ultimately Yeats's belief, faith, life, and art all became so inextricably intertwined with each other that it is utterly pointless to consider or discuss any one of them without reference to the others. For Yeats made the living of his life just as much an art as he did the writing of his poetry; he consciously viewed the shaping of his life and the shaping of his poetry as analogues of one another.

---

[16]Hoffman, 155.

Aiken and Yeats both always linked in their best work their efforts to shape their own lives and the composition of poetry. Out of the depths of their struggles with their hearts and souls emerged their best work. Both men believed in and participated in the struggle of the Romantics for enlarged consciousness and deepened emotions. In this matter they are at one with other modern Romantics like D. H. Lawrence, William Faulkner, and Herman Hesse.

Chapter 8

Visions of a Modern Romantic: Santayana, Nietzsche, and the Philosophic Mind

The modern poet working in the tradition of symbolism is partially and sometimes totally withdrawn from an urbanized world dominated by a reigning philosophy of positivism and by a pseudo-philosophy of journalistic slogans. Even when a symbolist like T. S. Eliot achieves a certain public stature as a statesman of modern letters, he hides his poetic self in his own abstruse language and convoluted thinking. The public thus sees only the shell of the poet, who remains invisible to all but a few comrades. Other poets, like Sandburg working in the tradition of Whitman, consciously seek large audiences, yet even in finding these audiences they too remain largely invisible as poets. Frost reading his work to an audience of a thousand at Harvard makes no more lasting poetic impression on large public audiences than Eliot reading to 14,000 at the University of Minnesota. Like Frost and Sandburg, Conrad Aiken in the twenties had hoped for a wide readership, for a literary success that his other two colleagues, as well as his friend Eliot, actually achieved. But by 1936, when he had begun to come to terms with both an inner and an outer chaos, Aiken had fully accepted his role as the modern invisible poet. Yet he still retained his inherited Romantic vision and, with a continued reading of his grandfather Potter's sermons, he became by the end of his life more deeply committed than in his younger years to many aspects of a nineteenth-century Transcendentalism that envisioned the remaking through the development of consciousness the whole of human society. Like Shelley, Aiken believed that the true poet must be an unacknowledged legislator in helping to reshape society.

Writing in the fifties and early sixties, Jay Martin links Aiken and his work to the nineteenth-century concept of the poet as sage and representative man, an idea put forth by Emerson in its most developed form. Linked to an Emersonian optimism, Martin says, is Aiken's own idea of "his function as a poet," which he stated in a critical essay of 1923 to the effect that "'art exists primarily for the fulfillment of an important social function.'" Thus the poet, Martin tells us, "orders and subtlizes his awareness so that he may deepen humanity's." This aspect of Aiken's work more than any other led to his revival in the sixties when both literary confession and personal and social improvement were highly valued. Martin's summing up of this side of Aiken's work makes a telling statement about the strongly "Romantic" tendencies of the sixties: "[I]n Aiken's work 'confession' is never present for its own sake--but is the material out of which he constructs the artifact that, he hopes, will benefit humanity."[1] In this sentence Martin links the concern of the New Criticism in the fifties with artistic form with the new Romanticism of the sixties.

Writing in the seventies, Malcolm Cowley stated that Aiken had in the beginning been poles apart from Emerson: "He had been atheistic and pessimistic, not optimistic and Unitarian." His intellectual models in his beginnings had been "Poe first of all, then Santayana, Freud, and Henry James," but, Cowley went on, "he had at the end of his long career . . . worked round to a position reminiscent of that which Emerson had reached in 1831, before he had published anything."[2] Cowley thus places Aiken in American literary history as a modern Romantic without noting that the poet had from his Harvard days been both pessimistic and optimistic, influenced as he was from his beginnings by the Romanticism of Whitman and by the modernism of the symbolists. Cowley does, however, correct Martin's portrait of Aiken as a representative man in the tradition described by John Holloway in his seminal book, *The Victorian Sage*, noting that Aiken would never have been comfortable in Emerson's Concord.

Using an intertextual method, Cowley shows how Aiken's major work grew out of Poe, James, Freud, and Santayana. What Cowley, however, fails to note is that there are two major intertextual traditions Aiken worked within. As I have already suggested, Aiken even as a child, needed Poe to launch himself into his own inner chaos. Later he would relate himself intertextually to Henry James in order to develop a philosophy based on heightened consciousness and the cultivation of the arts of civilization. What Cowley does not note is that the mature work of Aiken is most deeply related to that of Eliot. What these two friends and literary comrades drew from each other's works was the awareness of inner and outer chaos and with it the pilgrim's quest for a shamanistic vision that would help them to overcome the disintegrating powers within their own souls, powers that for years had

---

[1]Jay Martin, *Conrad Aiken: A Life of His Art* (Princeton: Princeton University Press, 1962), 203-204.

[2]Malcolm Cowley, "Conrad Aiken: From Savannah to Emerson," *The Southern Review* XI, no. 2 (Spring, 1975), 257.

threatened their very existence. Both poets also shared, at least in their early days at Harvard and afterwards in the twenties, an intertextual connection that was essentially philosophical. They would gradually diverge in their philosophical concerns as Eliot moved in the late twenties and thirties toward theology and Anglican ritual and as Aiken found it necessary to add to his early philosophical reading a deepening study of Freud and other depth psychologists. Finally, as Aiken turned toward America during and after World War II, leaving partly behind him his between-the-wars cosmopolitanism and its concern with an international modernism, he rediscovered his early Unitarian faith. Thus in order to see Aiken as both man and writer in the largest possible context it is necessary to examine his visionary life in terms of three major areas: the philosophical, the psychological, and the religious.

Aiken's earliest philosophical viewpoint was based on the scientific naturalism he encountered in his reading in the first decade of this century. This naturalism is found in his earliest published poems. Steven E. Olson has studied extensively the early work of Aiken and has discovered that even as a young man Aiken, the son of a doctor who was all his life a student of both the arts and the sciences, had read extensively in both the natural and the social sciences. Yet even as a naturalist Aiken did not accept the kind of scientific determinism that after 1900 was making great inroads into not only the social and natural sciences but also into American philosophy, which had earlier leaned heavily on an optimistic and idealistic view of the universe and that had emphasized the role of the individual in making conscious ethical decisions that could enhance both individual and collective life. This new determinism was often linked with the development of an analytic philosophy that grew out of nineteenth-century positivism. The chief failure of determinism, analytic philosophy, and positivism was that, as Victorino Tejara has pointed out, it "down-graded human nature." Also, Tejara goes on to say, "positivist philosophers of science have failed to take the human as a subject for observation."[3] Olson's study of the early Aiken reveals the poet's rejection of the new philosophical movements in America that would eventually enshrine deterministic, analytic, and positivistic thinking at the center of most American universities. Instead Aiken would follow the nineteenth-century philosophical interest in humankind's ethical nature. Aiken, Olson writes, "was one of the few artists of his generation to face the

---

[3]Victorino Tejara, *History as a Human Science* (Lanham, MD: University Press of America, 1984), 16.

exigencies of the modern age without rejecting the previous century's mandate that human existence can be understood in terms of conscious ethical purpose."[4] Aiken's early philosophical thinking had in a Renaissance fashion (he thought of his own father as a modern Renaissance man) sought to take into account the major fields of knowledge, the sciences as well as history, philosophy, and the arts. He even concerned himself with the popular culture of his day, including the comic strips and cinematic drama. But the centering of the young Aiken's thought in ethics was due primarily to the continuing influence of Harvard's most important philosopher, William James. To know the philosophical view that Aiken carried with him all his life one must know James and his relationship to Harvard.

The historian Page Smith has in his *Dissenting Opinions* described the ordeal of William James at Harvard. Now established in history as a classical American philosopher--possibly America's greatest--James was at turn-of-the-century Harvard an embattled man. Science, Smith tells us, had announced "a new methodology" and its advocates were seeking to "scientize" education. But a struggle arose over this attempted seizure of academic power. Smith thus continues the story of James at Harvard:

> The key figure in that struggle was William James, although there are a number of less well-known figures. Singlehandedly, James infused a substantial segment of Harvard with his enthusiasm for learning, for the things which 'enlighten and ennoble.' Starting off as a young instructor in anatomy, he moved in time to psychology, laying the foundation for that study, and then on to philosophy. With the somewhat bewildered support of Eliot [President Eliot of Harvard] he was able to attract a number of stars--Josiah Royce, sometimes Charles Sanders Pierce, George Santayana, and, finally, that Germanic oddity, Hugo Munsterberg.[5]

Smith describes James as a man who "refused to be overawed by the scientists" and as a "man who embodied humane learning" and who "made Harvard a fountainhead of intellectual energy." But even by the turn of the century "the game was pretty well lost. James was glad to retire." Thus, Smith continues, the "heavy-running tide of scientism" was too strong at last;

---

[4]Steven E. Olson, "The Vascular Mind: Conrad Aiken's Early Poetry, 1910-1918" (Ph.D. diss., Stanford University, 1981), 1.

[5]PageSmith, *Dissenting Opinions* (San Francisco: North Point Press, 1984), 113-114.

James was continually accused of lacking "objectivity" and, even worse, he "put too much of himself into his teaching and writing."[6] But James left behind him an important philosophical and poetic disciple to carry on the losing battle, George Santayana. As philosopher, poet, and novelist, Santayana would become the chief inspirer of the young Aiken at Harvard.

Aiken never took a course from James, but he was an eager reader of his work. Santayana, on the other hand, became a teacher, mentor, and lifelong friend. And the ways in which Santayana diverged in his thinking from James were particularly important for Aiken's development. Both men taught Aiken to honor the scientific enterprise without believing that the methodologies of scientism could take the place of authentic philosophy. James and Santayana were both personalists who in certain basic ways resembled Emerson, Henry James, Sr., and other nineteenth-century Transcendentalists. Tejara speaks of James's "spiritual inwardness within which he was raised as his father's son" and of the "intense inner lives" both William and his brother Henry lived.[7] Consciousness for James, as it was for Aristotle, Tejara tells us, "was not a substance but an activity." Aristotle believed that happiness was man's chief goal and that it was essentially an activity of the soul. For Santayana art and the contemplation of the arts were the chief ways in which the human being knew and expressed happiness. But, he wrote, "art will hardly be important or beautiful unless it engages deeply the resources of the soul."[8] Like James, Santayana believed that the development of consciousness was the most important single human activity and that the chief concern of education should be with this development. Santayana chiefly diverged from James in his exaltation of reason and art over the strictly moral and pragmatic concerns that were at the center of the Jamesian philosophy.

From the beginning of their association James had distrusted the aesthetic side of Santayana, and Santayana much later, in an essay on James, would attack his early mentor as one who denied the role of reason. For James, Santayana in his insistence on reason in the ancient Greek sense and in his exaltation of art was a man of the old and dying European culture. Both men were personalists in that they put the individual and his ability to make ethical choices at the center of their philosophy, but in matters of

---

[6]Ibid., 114.

[7]Tejara, 6.

[8]*The Philosopy of Santayana*, ed. Irwin Edman (New York: The Modern Library, 1936), 20-21.

metaphysics and religion there was basic disagreement. Santayana suggested that James's "radical empiricism and pragmatism were in his own mind only methods" and that "his doctrine" was "agnosticism." Therefore for James, Santayana says, religious faiths, not their objects, were the hard facts we must respect." The result was "no sense of security, no joy, in James's apology for personal religion. He did not really believe; he merely believed in the right of believing that you might be right if you believed."[9]

Santayana himself is often taken to be an agnostic. Morton White in discussing Santayana's philosophy writes that "he regards himself as an atheist and a Catholic" and that "He rejects the theology of Catholicism but rejoices in the poetry and the ritual of its religious ceremony."[10] Joy and rejoicing are indeed for Santayana marks of the philosopher who has gone to the heart of wisdom. The essential philosophical ingredient is the subject of his chief work of academic philosophy, *The Life of Reason*; it is a quality of the soul that the Greek philosophers and others who followed them called reason, the ability, that is, to perceive an underlying harmony in the universe. Santayana was agnostic in relationship to theism but was a believer in an essential element that made that activity of the soul called happiness possible. Santayana, summing up his basic concepts in "A Brief History of My Opinions," writes that "Harmony, which might be called an aesthetic principle, is also the principle of health, of justice, and of happiness." For Santayana, therefore, philosophizing meant the rational search for harmony in all human activities. In *The Life of Reason* he discusses at length such topics as "Reason in Society," "Reason in Art," and "Reason in Science." But for Santayana art is man's supreme activity: "Of all reason's embodiments art is therefore most splendid and complete."[11]

In studying under Santayana at Harvard, Aiken imbibed a viewpoint concerning joy, art, and harmony that would be for the rest of his life basic to his thought and literary activity. In his seventies Aiken talked to me at length of his experience of taking the course from Santayana that was based on a series of lectures that became *Three Philosophical Poets*, the book that more than any other continually reminded Aiken that his calling in life was to be a philosophical poet. Aiken once said that Eliot was also influenced by

---

[9]George Santayana, *Character and Opinion in the United States* (Garden City, New York: Doubleday and Co., 1956), 46-47.

[10]Morton White, *The Age of Analysis* (New York: The New American Library, 1955), 55.

[11]*The Philosophy of Santayana*, 224.

Santayana but later denied that influence. Santayana, a poet as well as a philosopher, undoubtedly, above all others at Harvard, planted the seeds of philosophical poetry in the two men. As Olson has written, Aiken "with T. S. Eliot, his friend and classmate . . . sought a new poetic voice, one in which one could think."[12]

Santayana was too much the maverick for Eliot, and finally too Romantic in his insistence on happiness as the human being's deepest need. Even at Harvard Eliot was caught up in guilt and in a kind of puritanical asceticism, whereas Aiken, less puritanical and in some ways more modern, would continue to search for joy as the chief ingredient in consciousness development. His next mentor, Freud, would also be searching for happiness and, fittingly, the man Aiken would turn to as the inspirer of the style and technique of his first novel. James Joyce would see great significance in the fact that his name Joyce should mean in Irish the same thing as the name Freud in German: joy. Consciousness for Santayana and Aiken could expand only through joy and love. Santayana's word for this expansion was *spirituality:* "Spirituality likes to say, Behold the lilies of the field! For its secret has the same simplicity as their vegetative art; only spirituality has succeeded in adding consciousness without confusing instinct."[13]

By exploring the meaning of love as well as of art, religion, and spirituality Santayana reveals a concern for basic human vision rather than for aestheticism or refined mental awareness in the narrow sense of these terms. Consciousness in the fullest sense meant for him the development of both the conscious mind and the intuitions and emotions. Only an apprehension of harmony could lead to this kind of development. Thus Santayana sums up his philosophical aims: "The intention of my philosophy has certainly been to attain, if possible, such wide intuitions, and to celebrate the emotions with which they fill the mind."[14] For Aiken the "evolution of consciousness" meant above all else an expansion of vision (Santayana's intuition) and of love. It is in this area--love and vision--as well as in the area of the uses of myth and ritual for expanding consciousness that Santayana, more than anyone else, pointed the way to Aiken and Eliot in their later endeavors to write philosophical poetry. White rightly says of Santayana's view of love that *The Life of Reason* contains "a sensible and sensitive

---

[12]Steven E. Olson, "The House of Man: Ethical Symbolism in Conrad Aiken's *The Clerk's Journal*," *Essays in Arts and Sciences* 13:2 (Fall, 1980), 25.

[13]*The Philosophy of Santayana,* 191.

[14]Ibid., 20.

recognition of the fact that love is animal in its basis and ideal in its aspiration" and that the "life of reason" reaches "its highest expression in religion, art, and science."[15] In spite of all the differences in their work Eliot and Aiken in their greatest philosophical poetry--the *Quartets* and the Preludes--reflect the views that the growth of love and vision is at the heart of the pilgrim's quest for the good life and that humanity is in fact moving on a path that will lead past the death of old cultures to a new idealism of shared existence. In other words, the bountiful hopes of Romantic and Victorian sages can be found, if searched for, in the best work of Aiken and Eliot. Santayana was the first of these sages that the two men knew personally, and his influence, often hidden, is present in crucial passages of their philosophical poetry.

Eliot hid even from himself the influence that Santayana had upon his work, but Aiken, on the other hand, found it necessary, shortly after leaving Harvard, to take up another, much different philosopher before he returned a few years later to the philosophical influence of his Harvard mentor. This philosopher was Friedrich Nietzsche. In 1913 in a letter to Grayson P. McCouch Aiken contrasts his viewpoint and that of John Masefield, whom he takes to be a disciple of Christ. Whereas Aiken, on the other hand, is rather a Nietzschean, with this difference that he does not believe in the development of the human race as the summum bonum, nor very much in anything except that he is alive and that life is beautiful.[16] By proclaiming that he believed in little if anything Aiken seems to be contradicting what he wrote to McCouch only a month earlier. McCouch had written that he did not care for the philosophy in an Aiken poem he had read, and Aiken had replied: "But for me, it was the philosophy that made the poem worth writing!" He goes on to say that he does not want to be as a writer "a pretty good kind of mirror." There ought to be something better, he says, and adds, "that is where my poor philosophy comes in." He then announces that he has in mind a whole cycle of tales, referring no doubt to the Symphonies, to be written "for the mere purpose of putting forth a very tangible philosophy of life *in terms of life itself.*"[17] The contradictions in the above passages can partly be explained in terms of Aiken's own debunking spirit; the poet is kicking up his heels after release from an academic discipline at Harvard that

---

[15] *The Age of Analysis*, 54-55.

[16] *Selected Letters of Conrad Aiken*, edited by Joseph Killorin (New Haven: Yale University Press, 1978), 32-33.

[17] Ibid., 23-24.

he sometimes found demoralizing. Nevertheless, there is stated in these early letters a philosophical viewpoint that Aiken would maintain all his life because he could never accept the remote, academic, thought-ridden stance of a man like Santayana. Like Eliot calling into question his own academic mentors in "East Coker," Aiken often questioned the academic philosophical viewpoint as being too remote from life. In his life and work he is continually deconstructing the kind of ordered, speculative thought he found in Santayana and other Harvard professors.

In stating that he wanted to write in order to put forth a "very tangible philosophy of life *in terms of life itself*" Aiken takes an existential position before the term existentialism was even invented. In turning to Nietzsche, who along with Kierkegaard is regarded as a creator of existentialism, Aiken found a serious thinker who had left academic philosophy, which he only in part understood, to become a kind of Romantic prophet who accepted the rigors of ordinary existence as something the real philosopher in an apocalyptic age must do if his work is to mean anything. In that book in which Nietzsche launches his profoundest attack on academic philosophy, *Beyond Good and Evil*, the German philosopher makes clear the distinction between academic philosophers like Kant and Hegel, whom he calls the philosophical specialists, and true philosophers like himself. The academic wisdom is thus defined: "Wisdom: that seems to the populace to be a kind of flight, a means and artifice for withdrawing successfully from a bad game." But "the *genuine* philosopher," one like himself, Nietzsche says, "lives unphilosophically" and "unwisely," above all, *"imprudently,"* and "feels the obligation and burden of a hundred attempts and temptations of life--he risks *himself* constantly, he plays *this* bad game [Nietzsche's emphasis]."[18] Aiken realized throughout his life that risk-taking was necessary for both his life and work, and for him the greatest risks were with friends like Eliot, Lowry, and Fletcher and with wives who could be, like Lorenz, necessary Lorelei to draw him into domestic tranquility or sexual encounter. Like Nietzsche, Aiken believed that the "genuine" philosopher had to pass a large number of life's tests to be accounted truly philosophical. The term genuine, or authentic as we see it rendered in English, became a catchword for existential philosophers in the twentieth-century because most of them assumed that they were clearing away, in an apocalyptic age, the debris of academic thinking in order to make way for a philosophy based

---

[18]Friedrich Nietzsche, *Beyond Good and Evil*, translated by Helen Zimmern (Chicago: Henry Regnery Co., 1952), 136.

firmly on lived experience. The total experience of intense individuals is for Aiken and most existentialists the central fact of human life and not the abstract thinking so highly praised by academic philosophers.

Yet for Aiken Nietzsche was the great philosopher for only a few years after leaving Harvard. The reason is that he turned again to his Romantic roots and took up Santayana again as his guiding philosopher when, in 1917 with "Tetelestai," he launched his first poems of pilgrimage, poems that grew in part out of his reading of both Santayana and Freud. These poems mark the beginning of his major work. His first volume, *Earth Triumphant* (1914), written in his Nietzschean days, Aiken refused to include in his canon. Santayana and Freud were necessary for Aiken's conscious philosophizing, as Nietzsche was not, because the poet had to have an initiatory guide into his own tormented psyche (Freud) and another guide (Santayana) who spoke the modern accents of an earlier branch of Romanticism that proclaimed the possibility of a personal and social growth that involved love, harmony, and joy. Thus the evolution of consciousness for Aiken, after his exposure to Santayana's class from which *Three Philosophical Poets* emerged, meant an evolution of humanity in the direction of love, joy, and imaginative awareness. And indeed Santayana was reinforcing Aiken's reading in Wordsworth and Shelley. At the end of *Three Philosophical Poets* Santayana writes of "a second form of rational art" after mentioning a first form that "may come to buttress a particular form of life, or. . . may come to express it." This form "expresses the ideal towards which we would move under these improved conditions." The improved conditions Santayana refers to are those whereby a new art based on a rational philosophy of the sort Santayana professed could emerge. The result, he says at the end of the book, would be "to establish a new religion and a new art, based on moral liberty and moral courage." Thus Santayana calls for a new poet similar to Shelley's unacknowledged legislator: "It is time some genius should appear to reconstitute the shattered picture of the world."[19] Aiken did not take himself to be the supreme poetic genius who would perform the shamanic task of presenting a new harmonious picture of the world, in a new and powerful language. Rather, he saw himself as one of many artists and thinkers working together in the evolution of human consciousness so that, as certain creative individuals continued to develop, a new visionary awareness could in time emerge. Thus the artists of an age to follow the

---

[19]George Santayana, *Three Philosophical Poets* (Garden City, New York: Doubleday and Co., 1953), 189-190.

modern apocalypse would give the world visions of harmony and love that would shape life itself to an ideal end.

Santayana therefore provided Aiken with hope for a new art and with both ethical and metaphysical principles with which to work for the eventual triumph of that art. The ethics of Santayana pointed to the courage and free choice of the individual to search out and to find the way of life for himself whereby he could develop his own consciousness and help to develop the consciousness of others. Aiken's view of politics would grow out of this ethical view, which advocated a continuing exercise of free choice. For Aiken, he says at the end of *Ushant*, real political and social change can occur only through the growth of the consciousness of individuals who coalesce and thus through that cohesiveness form the basis for the sharing of those values necessary to undergird authentic human culture. The metaphysical insight provided by Santayana was that of an essential cosmic harmony that could be found both in the good society and in the universe, a harmony that the pilgrim must seek and find.

This pilgrim for Aiken is "divine" because he seeks the one enduring element, harmony, which expresses itself in human affairs as love. Aiken's use of the concept of harmony is essentially the same as that of Yeats' use of unity as a basic concept. Both figures are in the tradition of major nineteenth-century sages, Matthew Arnold, for instance, or Emerson, or Wordsworth. These earlier sages also believed that to encounter harmony was to experience emotions like love and joy, which are necessary for the renewing of society. These are the healing emotions that Arnold believed Wordsworth taught his jaded readers to recover.

Even in the same month that Aiken was proclaiming himself a Nietzschean to McCouch, he was stating in a letter to Eliot a belief straight out of Romanticism concerning a poetry that would bring forth emotions that would "seek a practical end." Thus he writes:

At least, poetry justifies itself, pour moi, only in so far as it is philosophic. Mere wanton poetry seems to me both foolish and morbid. Only those emotions are healthy which in some way seek a practical: emotion per se (as A. P. Baker is fond of saying, pronounced pursee) is a bastard thing, bad both for the author and the reader, for with both it is only a substitute for actual experience.[20]

---

[20] *Selected Letters of Conrad Aiken*, 30.

Aiken distinguishes here between love and a sentimentalism that marks withdrawal from the pain of shared existence. His "healthy" emotions both then and throughout his life would be the love that makes individual and social growth through creative interaction possible. In the major poetry of Eliot and Aiken--the *Quartets* and the Preludes in particular--the very necessity of love for meaningful existence is made clear. The great philosophical link between the two poets is their expression of harmony in terms of music. For both men music was the chief symbol--as was the dance for Yeats--of a harmony that must be discovered if love is to be experienced. Helen Hagenbuechle cites Aiken's continuing concern with music as central to his philosophical viewpoint: "His preoccupation with musical structure in poetry is at the same time an epistemological concern. His search for a style is also, and above all, a quest for truth."[21] Truth, of course, is in modern philosophy a term that invites deconstruction whenever it appears in speculation. But what Hagenbuechle really means is that Aiken conducted a philosophical quest for a metaphysical principle that would, if adhered to, yield the two emotions he believed were necessary for life itself--love and joy.

It is not so much truth that Aiken wants but emotions that he believes to be the foundation for a continuing human existence. The affirmation of harmony--particularly as it is seen in music and poetry--brings forth in Aiken the required emotions. In accepting the reality of these emotions Aiken follows in the footsteps of William James, whose philosophy was based on an ethical pragmatism. But as Santayana noted in his essay on James, the great pragmatist believed in no metaphysical principle and therefore had no way of evaluating the so-called "cash value" of his applied philosophy. A. N. Whitehead in *Science and the Modern World* wrote that any philosophy to be complete must have a *summum bonum*, in essence a basic metaphysical principle. Santayana helped to supply Aiken with a *summum bonum*--cosmic harmony--and the poet clung to it all his life, but with modifications.

Aiken's modifications are related to two different philosophical movements he little understood because of a lack of reading in the subjects and to a movement called in his time depth psychology, which he understood well and that he helped through his work to promote. Aiken seems strange as an artist and thinker to many contemporary minds because he at once held

---

[21]Helen Hagenbuechle, "Epistemology and Musical Form in Conrad Aiken's Poetry," *Studies in the Literary Imagination*, Vol. 13, no. 2 (Fall 1980), 25.

to basic Romantic ideas like harmony, love, and joy and to the modern vision of fragmentation, decay and lovelessness. His own existentialism, like Nietzsche's, sprang from a need to rise above decay and psychic pain. Like Nietzsche, who was both a romantic and a modernist, he wanted to rise above the collapse of world culture and affirm a great new age of the transformed individual. For Nietzsche the new age was symbolized by the "superman." For Aiken the man of evolved conscience was the goal of human striving and the types of the higher man for Aiken were Freud and Socrates, men unafraid of experiencing the life around them with all its ugliness. In looking forward to a new age both Aiken and Nietzsche were Romantics, and in wanting to experience a "joyful wisdom," to use Nietzsche's term, they were both Romantic and existential. They were both modern in accepting the horror of disintegration, which the total Romantic, even those in this century like D. H. Lawrence, Dylan Thomas, Malcolm Lowry, or Hart Crane want to ignore or flee. The two men in their own different ways were mediators between Romanticism and modernism.

Nietzsche and Aiken were also deconstructionists in that they both attacked logocentric aspects of philosophy and theology, though Nietzsche's work as deconstructionist was far more sweeping. Jacques Derrida has accepted Nietzsche, and Nietzsche's chief philosophical disciple Heidegger, as mentors because these two men had what might be the most powerful deconstructive minds in European history. For Nietzsche the chief European system to be decomposed is a Platonized Christianity. Thus Nietzsche writes: "But the struggle against Plato . . . the struggle against the ecclesiastical oppression of millenniums of Christianity (for Christianity is Platonism for the 'people'), produced in Europe a magnificent tension of soul."[22] To use Derrida's terms, Nietzsche found a Platonized Christianity whose *logocentricity* denied the *difference* that springs from human freedom. Earlier the first existentialist, Kierkegaard, had deconstructed an Hegelianized Christianity as too abstract for human needs because it imprisoned in "ideas" the subjective aspect of human existence. Derrida's *difference* is an undefinable, even mystical principle, but surely it is connected with the unique subjective self of the individual. Aiken's own deconstruction sprang directly from the writer who, after Schopenhauer, most inspired Nietzsche, Ralph Waldo Emerson. Emerson and his philosophical follower Whitman demanded the end of creeds and dogmas--the end of all abstractions and a return to nature as symbol of cosmic wholeness and a loving acceptance of

---

[22]*Beyond Good and Evil*, 2.

all individuals. Aiken in his work also deconstructed creeds and dogmas, but unlike the nineteenth-century predecessors whom he followed--Emerson, Whitman, and Nietzsche among others--Aiken did not set himself up as a prophet who stood on a lonely intellectual mountain top. Instead he took a more humble route of pilgrim and literary comrade. Nevertheless, the deconstructing aspects of his work, linked as they are to his occasional visions of nothingness, undergird one of the most complex philosophical visions in American literature.

Aiken's deconstruction of the logocentric aspects of Christianity as well as of philosophy and literary criticism is a powerful modern element in his work. But the strongest modern element in Aiken is taken from Freud and other depth psychologists. And while holding on to his philosophical base in Romanticism, which he derived from Wordsworth, Emerson, William James, and Santayana, he lived most of his adult life as a writer committed to the study of modern depth psychology, one who readily admitted and even studied at length his own psychic problems. Out of this study and the incorporation of its results in his work Aiken came round early in his career to a fully modern kind of existentialist viewpoint in which he accepted his own and other's subjectivity with an awareness of human faults and virtues. And, particularly through his reading of Alfred Adler, he achieved an awareness of what the French existentialist Gabriel Marcel called intersubjectivity, which for many modern existentialists means the acceptance of other individuals in terms of their own subjectivity and in terms of the lived experience of their times. Aiken was largely unread in existentialist thinkers, but, as I have demonstrated in a book-length study of Aiken and Walker Percy, Aiken's life followed distinctive patterns found in the work of various authors who work within the existentialist tradition. Subjectivity and intersubjectivity as filtered through the thinking of Freud, Adler, Jung, and other depth psychologists are therefore categories that must be considered in the philosophical development of Conrad Aiken. What now must be examined is the way that Aiken's involvement in the study of depth psychology from his earliest creative period until the end of his life was a spur to new philosophical and religious exploration after his permanent settlement in America.

Chapter 9

Immanence and Transcendence

In the development of his philosophical and theological views Conrad Aiken passed through three distinct periods. The first period saw the development of a basic philosophical viewpoint derived in part from William James and George Santayana as well as from his many learned associations at Harvard and in Boston. The second period in the years between the wars saw a marked turn to Europe and to Freudian psychology as well as other civilizations of the world, some, like Egypt, of the remote past. In Boston Aiken had felt the pull of Freud and other depth psychologists, and there he was also drawn to the work of the Egyptologist Flinders Petrie, eventually employing knowledge of ancient Egypt to formulate a view of man that was deeper than any he had discovered in America. The third period saw the dominance of the thought of his maternal grandfather, William James Potter. Santayana was predominant in Aiken's early thought whereas depth psychology became the major source of his worldview between the wars. After 1939, the big event in Aiken's life was the rediscovery of his American past; at the same time his religious views deepened, becoming partly associated with the religion of his maternal grandfather. As a result Aiken developed a deconstructed Protestant viewpoint that was in some ways quite different from, and in other ways very similar to, the American Transcendentalism that, according to Jay Martin and Malcolm Cowley, Aiken eventually accepted as his own religion.

Aiken and his third wife, Mary Hoover, did not in 1939 return to America with any eagerness. By the 1930s Aiken had clearly become a transatlantic writer going back and forth between the literary circles of London, Boston, and New York. Yet Aiken, always the mediator between the city and nature, preferred to live in the small English town of Rye, where he occupied his beloved Jeake's House. But the outbreak of World War II in 1939 forced the Aikens to move back to America. As Joseph Killorin puts it, "The prospect of making ends meet, especially as impoverished aliens in wartime England who might not be allowed to live in coastal Rye, decided Conrad Aiken and Mary to sail--reluctantly--on September 29 for New York and the cheaper living of Cape Cod."[1] Although Aiken and his wife would return to Jeake's House after the war, they would, until Aiken died in 1973, be associated mainly with two houses: the inherited family home, Forty-One Doors on Stony Brook Road in Brewster, Massachusetts and, after 1962, the Regency House on Oglethorpe Avenue in Savannah that stood next to the house when he had lived as a child. He would spend two years, from 1945 to 1947, mainly at Jeake's House in Rye but would sell it in 1947 and become at last a permanent resident in America, maintaining a small apartment in New York, which he and Mary visited several times a year. After 1962 the Aikens wintered in Savannah until 1972 when the various illnesses of the author (a skin disease and a heart condition) made it impossible to return to Brewster. As always in his life, the particular place where Aiken happened to be living had a profound influence on his work. The spirit of place always played a significant role in the development of his art and his beliefs concerning God and humanity. New found beliefs concerning his own inherited religious background, more than any other beliefs, would help to shape the religious views of the final period of his life.

Throughout the 1930s Aiken, though still primarily an expatriate in England, was putting down new roots in America. His first two volumes after World War II--*The Kid* (1947) and *Skylight One: Fifteen Poems* (1949)--were, as Killorin notes, "fruit of 'that powerful seed of conversion' to his New England heritage, lodged in him by his discovery of William Blackstone in 1925 and again, while working on the *Massachusetts Guide*, in 1937."[2] Both volumes are important for what they reveal of the evolution of Aiken's view of America. *The Kid* seeks, as Harry Marten writes, to embrace "the myths and dreams on which the western movement was based and the harsher, sometimes humorous realities of the frontier."[3] Though a minor work, *The Kid* contains a major Aiken theme, that of the struggles of pioneers both of the material and spiritual realms to open up new territory for humanity. Walt Whitman, for instance, is one of the incarnations of this prototype of the American pioneer. Thus Aiken acknowledges late in his career just how much he has in common with the greatest poet of the American Transcendentalist movement just as, in the 1950s, he would

---

[1]Joseph Killorin, "Conrad Aiken's Use of Autobiography,"*Studies in the Literary Imagination* 13, 2 (Fall, 1980), 31.

[2]Ibid., 43.

[3]Harry Marten, "The Unconquerable Ancestors: 'Mayflower,' 'The Kid,' 'Halloween,'" *Studies in the Literary Imagination* 13, 2 (Fall, 1980), 58.

celebrate Herman Melville as a "mariner of the human soul" who "loved the Whale." Douglas Robillard points out that this salute to Melville in the poem "Herman Melville," included in the volume *Sheepfold Hill* (1958), is "celebratory, but is personal, too, for here more than anywhere else in his writings Aiken seems to be touching upon those qualities in Melville that he himself found of most lasting value."[4] Thus from "Mayflower" in 1945 on through *The Kid* in 1947, and "Hallowe'en" and *Sheepfold Hill* in 1958, Aiken not only established once again his American roots but he also reaffirmed his connections with important American precursors who had helped to point him the way toward the concept of the divine pilgrimage and had helped to sustain him in the postwar period when Romanticism was more than ever under attack from the New Critics.

The idea that a poet might be expressing his own deeply felt metaphysical beliefs increasingly seemed absurd to most New Critics, in spite of the fact that the acknowledged dean of this critical movement, Allen Tate, wrote from deeply held metaphysical views of his own. In the 1950s form became a kind of idol for young New Critics as the deep structure of language would later become the central belief of structuralists. But consistently throughout the period from 1945 to the present the subject of literature in relationship to belief would be discussed in terms of Wallace Stevens's idea of the "supreme fiction" (and some of Aiken's poems can certainly be seen in this light) or, later, in terms of what Harold Bloom in *A Map of Misreading* would call "the beautiful lie of the Imagination." Only among critics who retained a sense of biography and literary criticism would there be continuing concern for the artist's creation of an artifact that reflected his own metaphysical vision based on personal belief. The best known Aiken critic of the 1970s, Malcolm Crowley, would, in fact, center a significant study of Aiken's work on his personal development.

In "Conrad Aiken: From Savannah to Emerson," a *Southern Review* article of 1975 that was later included in--*And I Worked at the Writer's Trade* (1978), Cowley traces the upsurge of Transcendentalism that appears in Aiken's work after 1939. "Hallowe'en" is in part a dialogue with grandfather Potter; in this poem Aiken through his dialogue with Potter resolves personal difficulties he faced in the late forties. For Cowley the most important aspect of Aiken's belief is to be found in a section from Potter's journal that he quotes in the poem. When Aiken read Potter's published

---

[4]Douglas Robillard, "Conrad Aiken and Herman Melville," *Studies in the Literary Imagination* 13, no. 2 (Fall, 1980), 95.

sermons, Cowley says, he was "impressed by their bold speculations about the divine element in men." A quoted phrase in "Hallowe'en" from Potter that Cowley pinpoints states the immanent view of God that the Transcendentalists generally held: "[S]o man may make the god finite and viable, make conscious god's power in action and being."[5] Citing the microcosm-macrocosm concept in Transcendentalism as well as the doctrine of the correspondence between tangible things and the mind, Cowley notes that Aiken in his last years returned to Emerson. He thus seconds Harry Marten's belief that Aiken inherited Emersonian Transcendentalism more directly than almost any other modern poet. This is, in one sense, correct, yet Unitarians by the nature of their basic beliefs have all differed greatly in the details of their religion. In 1965 Aiken freely admitted to me that he was a Unitarian. He also expressed sorrow that Eliot had become an Anglican and that Harvard in its general view of religion had moved from Unitarianism to Anglicanism. Yet Aiken also suggested in remarks to me and to others that his Unitarianism was highly individualistic, was, in fact, his own and not Emerson's or Potters's. In his own mind he remained until the end of his life a spiritual pioneer as well as a priest of consciousness, and, as such, there was nothing in his work or life that indicates he "went back" to Emerson or Potter. Instead, as with Santayana and Freud, he used Potter, and to a lesser extent Emerson, to move forward on his own continuing pilgrimage, which at least since the twenties had been a lifetime progression.

Cowley views Aiken's last book-length poem, *Thee*, as Transcendentalist and points out an Emerson poem that Aiken had not read but that is in some ways similar to Aiken's poem. *Thee* contains references to the immanent nature of God characteristic of the American Transcendentalist tradition, yet the major fact of the poem is its primary emphasis on a transcendent God, who is for Aiken at the same time immanent. Questioning Aiken about the poem in 1968 (it was published in 1967 and has received little attention), I discovered that the poet himself thought of *Thee* as primarily a struggle with and questioning of God very much in the Old Testament tradition of Job or of Jacob as Israel, the wrestler with a divine emanation. Aiken assured me that God in the end won the match. There are also in his work earlier examples of the poet struggling with God as transcendent being. For instance, in *The Kid*, he writes: "Working and weeping, Lord, I defy Thee./ In hurt and injustice I know and deny Thee" *(CP*, 863). Yet at the close of this passage, written for Brooks

---

[5]Ibid., 251.

Adams in the poem, Aiken typically cites terror and horror as central facts of existence and then proclaims, in terms of his own aesthetic heroism, that he at once receives and changes God: "Come terror, come horror, no need to escape Thee:/ dipped in my death, I receive Thee and shape Thee!" (*CP*, 862). Before he begins his address to a transcendent deity, Aiken makes an indirect reference to the dying and resurrected God of world mythology: "the invisible sighted, invisibly slain,/ and darkly, in blood, resurrected again" (*CP* 862). In several of Aiken's best religious poems, notably "Tetélestai" and "The Poet in Granada," the dying god becomes specifically Christ, and the supreme God that is suggested reminds us in part at least of the transcendent God of the Judeo-Christian tradition.

My own various studies of Aiken's religious symbolism have shown that the poet often invokes both Christ and a transcendent God when recalling early traumatic experiences as a kind of preparatory school outcast in Savannah and later in Massachusetts,. Thus some of his best work is based on his awareness of psychological pain. For instance, in "Changing Mind," the poem that more than any other launched Aiken's Preludes (poems in which the transcendent deity is many times invoked), Christ is an essential part of the poet's discovery of his inner being. After proclaiming in "Changing Mind" his own daily death through the continuing killing of Narcissus, the poet discovers that both Christ and Socrates dwell within him and that a scene of a daily crucifixion exists on a Golgotha within his soul. Thus Aiken as pilgrim describes himself as one who, though always sick and weak, fights against the threatening shadow forces: "Daily I fight here,/ Daily I die for the world's delight/ By the giant blow on my visible heart!" (*CP*, 287).

Furthermore, the collection that completes Aiken's major poetic effort of the thirties, *Brownstone Ecologues and Other Poems* (1942), is possibly the most religiously oriented of all of his work. The first poem, "Sursum Corda" is, as Frederick J. Hoffman tells us, "one of the great modern commentaries on the Christ symbol." Its emphasis, Hoffman suggests, "is upon the human implication (complicity) in the death of Christ."[6] Yet in spite of the merits of the poem, its references to Christ lack the power similar references have in earlier works like "Tetélestai" and *Blue Voyage*, both of which record Aiken's own struggle with his sense of inner chaos. The chief value of the poems of this most important volume of the 1940s is its evocation of the shabby side of the American city and the sense of failure

---

[6]Frederick J. Hoffman, *Conrad Aiken* (New York: Twayne, 1962), 67.

and defeat experienced everyday by its inhabitants. Yet, as the poem "Saint Ambrose: Early Morning" records, an intrusion of God both in transcendent and immanent manifestations is still possible even for urbanized sceptics: "Or even a little love; or, out of stillness,/ a blinding apocalypse!" (*CP*, 782).

In *Brownstone Ecologues* Aiken sometimes adopts the attitude of prayer, as he does in other works which record his sense of his own and other people's suffering. In "Saint Ambrose: Early Morning" Aiken associates the unhappiness of the city with an instinctive reaching out in prayer to a higher power: "alas, the whole city's unhappy, unspoken words,/ one vast and ragged prayer" (*CP*, 781). Prayer as invocation of a transcendent power is the basis of "Stone Too Can Pray":

> Lord, Lord--all voices say, and all together, weather--
> stone, steel, and waking man, and waking
> give us thy day, that once more we may be
> the endless miracle that embodies thee (*CP*, 812)

The collection's last poem echoes the idea of humanity as "endless miracle" by proclaiming that immorality and "Victory's heart had ceased to be a tombstone;/ and death, forever, world without end, a failure" (*CP*, 813). Along with Aiken's rediscovery of the shabby side of American cities, there is in *Brownstone Ecologues* the same kind of apocalyptic awareness that we see in his best work of the thirties. The pain of war thus accompanies the awareness of urban blight, both spiritual and physical, which Aiken discovered in cities like Boston and New York.

That Aiken was closely attuned to the general reactions of America to World War II can be seen in a poem published two years after *Brownstone Ecologues* that is generally thought to be a failure, *The Soldier: A Poem* (1944). Instead of prayer he offers the modern warrior a sense of his own past as soldier and points at the end of the poem to the ultimate war everyone must fight if he is to be fully human:

> In the last war of all
> we conquer ourselves. Look home from the desert, soldier;
> to the regenerate desert of the heart come home:
> and know that this too needs heroes and endurance, and
> 　　　　　　　　ardour (*CP*, 843).

Although similar in some way to *Brownstone Ecologues*, the end of *The Soldier* marks a turning away from both a sense of apocalypse and of a strong invocation of Christ and the transcendent Judeo-Christian God that is a significant part of the period between 1929 and 1945. At the end of *The Soldier* Aiken seems to be emphasizing once again the human heart and the human necessity of discovering its reality in emotional terms and its true relationship to the Self within. Aiken thus prepared himself and others who read him for the aftermath of World War II, when the inner struggle of the pilgrim would again be the chief work of those aspired to be modern heroes.

After *The Soldier* Aiken also entered a new phase of his philosophical life, a phase that is described in his *Paris Review* interview, to the effect that he was continuing the work of his Grandfather Potter. What he greatly admired about Potter, he said, was his "determined acceptance of Darwin and all the rest of the scientific fireworks of the nineteenth century."[7] Furthermore, he makes the point that Potter believed everyone could become a god. Potter's emphasis on his views about science and immanence, God as the center of human existence in terms of the Self, would inevitably raise the question of how Aiken, as one who speaks of himself as a believer in a kind of Transcendentalist immanence, could also be a theist who affirms a transcendent God. The answer to this question, I think, can be found in the full acceptance of a variety of religious experiences (remember William James's use of this term) which, though seeming different, are all linked to the fact of pilgrimage as Aiken saw this process.

It is fitting that his last great poem, "A Letter from Li Po," written in the 1950s, should be based on the work of a Chinese poet who could comfortably live at once with several religions. For centuries the Japanese and Chinese have found it possible to be, without contradiction, a Buddhist on one occasion and a Shintoist or Taoist on another. Potter's vision for religion in the future was that it would be worldwide and devoid of dogma because its participants were at one in gazing at the divine harmony underlying all existence. Thus E. P. Bollier sums up Aiken's vision in "A Letter from Li Po": "West meets East, the world is circumnavigated, mankind becomes one, the living and dead, both mortal and immortal at once."[8] Aiken in "A Letter from Li Po" thus sums up that aspect of the

---

[7]*Writers at Work: The Paris Review Interviews*, Third Series (New York: Viking Press, 1966), 183.

[8]E. P. Bollier, "Conrad Aiken's Ancestral Voices: A Reading of Four Poems," *Studies in the Literary Imagination* 13 (Fall, 1980), 69.

shamanic belief that Mircea Eliade has called the yearning for paradise, the search, that is, for a unified paradisiacal world. A few artists and religious figures throughout the world retain this vision in their consciousness, Aiken believed, and through their work on behalf of the evolution of consciousness, he taught, they prepare for that historical era when the visionary life and the fully developed heart will be the central facts of existence.

Aiken's continuation of the work of Potter after World War II would consist in part in exploring his own immanent and transcendent experiences of deity, and in his specifically religious poetry he would incorporate mystical and speculative elements that would define basic Unitarian and Transcendentalist positions that he held. Aiken, I think, understood Potter's original religious position that had led his grandfather to reject Unitarianism as a church because the sect in New England had considered some rites and beliefs more important than others and had finally decided to consider itself a Christian denomination. Born a Quaker, Potter had felt the Friends were, as Cowley puts it, "too confining." Of Potter's career, Cowley tells us that in 1866 he refused to administer the rite of communion: "following the example of Emerson, he told his congregation that he could no longer do so in good conscience" and in 1867 "he refused to call himself a Christian and was thereupon dropped from the role of Unitarian ministers." Potter, however, was admired "for being upright and unselfish and a good preacher" and "his congregation gave him a unanimous vote of confidence." I quote Cowley to illustrate certain differences between Potter and Emerson, who together with a group founded the Free Religious Association, which, in Cowley's words, "was intended to unite all religions of the world by rejecting their dogmas and retaining from each faith only its ethical core. Dogmas were what he [Potter] abhorred."[9] Emerson and Potter differed from each other in Potter's continuing participation in a religious community and in Emerson's own growing isolation, expressed for instance, by Lewis P. Simpson in an essay, "Emerson's Early Thought": "Family, friends, servants--all fade as the Self in the flow of the currents of the Universal Being becomes part and parcel of God. The flow of Being is away from the human community."[10]

Aiken, Potter, and Emerson all share a Transcendentalist tradition, a Unitarian tradition, and even a renegade Unitarian tradition. Yet because all

---

[9]Cowley, 252.

[10]Lewis P. Simpson, *The Man of Letters in New England and the South* (Baton Rouge: Louisiana State University Press, 1973), 83.

three traditions were essentially deconstructionist in their attitudes toward doctrine and ritual, they all inevitably contained private and unique views of deity and human existence. Anabaptists, Quakers, Socinians, Swedenborgians, some early Methodists, and other extreme Protestant groups in the seventeenth and eighteenth centuries were busily deconstructing the complex edifice of inherited classical theology bequeathed them by the medieval Church; Transcendentalists, Swedenborgians, and Unitarians have continued working in this tradition even to the present. Deconstructionists in all periods of history have had various ends in mind. Some in our time, like certain Communists and radical feminists, deconstruct both the human being and his ideologies in order to establish nihilistic or hedonistic viewpoints. The early religious deconstructionists sought to overthrow logocentrism by getting rid of dogma and by enshrining human uniqueness (the difference) at the center of religious practice. They retained, as Cowley says, the "ethical core" of religion but not logocentric systems of morality. They also kept the metaphysical concept of a divine ground, seen by Emerson in terms of Self (soul) and Oversoul. In New England, in particular, the seventeenth-century concept of pilgrimage was retained by many Transcendentalists and Unitarians.

Aiken was always at heart a Unitarian Transcendentalist, but on his own, with the help mainly of Santayana and Freud, he had to rediscover his own soul and the pilgrim's life in the twentieth century. What he discovered in his life and work was the need to face over and over both death and destructive emotion, within and without. Above all, he early experienced the isolation Emerson knew all his life and could never face fully. Both grandfather and grandson also needed and found a community of people; for Aiken this community consisted of poets and other artists who thought the way he did. Yet Aiken never knew the kind of communal stability Potter experienced in nineteenth-century Massachusetts. But through a long pilgrimage he came at last to have various small mystical experiences of the sort Transcendentalists and some Unitarians were once noted for, and he recorded these experiences, along with certain of his dreams, in a poetry that for many still seems old fashioned. Yet in that part of his poetry that anticipates much contemporary verse he could express his own deconstructed religious insights. Of Aiken's particular insight into Self and language ("the self becoming word, the word/ becoming world") Bollier says:

If self and world as absolutes each are a one, the only possible square root of each is 'one,' and 'one' multiplied by itself *ad infinitum* results always in 'one.' Self and world, then, are multiplied series or succession of ones. Mathematical metaphor, of course, can take us only so far, but what Aiken intends, I think, is to affirm that each self is a unique point of convergence of a potentially infinite number of other singular selves.[11]

Thus Aiken, Bollier tells us, has established the concept of human uniqueness, or difference in Derrida's sense of that aspect of humanity that defies all logocentricity. Yet Aiken's self, as he continually proclaims in the Preludes and on through his last poems, is also God in some way that is beyond definition. But then, as Aiken makes clear in *Ushant,* that quintessence of existence that must continually be sought is always beyond analysis or rational definition.

Aiken's religious position as I have defined it is far more complex than anything Potter or Emerson, themselves theological deconstructionists in their own century, could have imagined. Part of that complexity lies in the mysterious aspect that death and chaos, relatively unimportant categories in early Transcendentalism, played in Aiken's religious vision. Aiken, in fact, resembles Heidegger in his use of these categories more than he does either Emerson or Potter. Aiken, if anything, resembles, far more than he does earlier figures, the contemporary American philosopher William Barrett, whose work he never encountered but whose book of the late1970s, *The Illusion of Technique,* reminds us in many ways of Aiken's deepest philosophical and religious viewpoints. Like Aiken, Barrett has roots in the nineteenth-century Transcendental tradition, and some critics, because of his emphasis on ethical choice, nature, and individualism, have called Barrett an Emersonian. But just as Aiken had learned from Freud to encounter the instinctive and irrational aspects of existence in order to find himself, so Barrett discovered in Heidegger, as a disciple and as a philosophical specialist in the study and teaching of the German philosopher, the wisdom concerning the necessary encounter with death and chaos, both personal and social, that is required to achieve authentic existence. Thus Barrett sums up this aspect of Heidegger: "Dasein's story is this: He is thrown into the world, and loses himself in its various external trivia; but through the encounter with death in the light of his own extreme possibility that death discloses to him, he may rise to the level of an authentic existence. He may even become

---

[11]Bollier, 67.

aware of the unique authentic sense in which his existence is historical, and so play a free and authentic part in the historical mission of his time."[12]

As a student of Heidegger, Derrida himself establishes his almost mystical idea of difference on the sense of the unique that Heidegger believes is the result of the facing of death. But as an American rooted in Emerson and even more in William James, Barrett cannot finally accept Heidegger's definition of human beings as Dasein--"being in a particular, historical place." He accepts Heidegger's concept of Being in its historical context and Heidegger's belief in the encounter with death, but there came a time in his studying and teaching of Heidegger, Barrett tells us, when there seemed "something strangely empty about this Dasein." Then he writes: "[T]he words that expressed it came spontaneously and forced themselves upon me, and they were these: 'Dasein has no soul.'"[13] It is the plunge into one's own soul, Barrett tells us, that gives an individual a sense of what William James meant by the moral will. The Jamesian ethical sense is not based on a choice related to a logocentric ethical system but is rather a choice that leads to confrontation with the creative powers within the soul. Thus summing up his own perception of the Jamesian ethical will, Barrett writes: "Perhaps the will, at its deepest, does not connote self-assertion and dominance, but love and acquiescence; not the will to power but the will to prayer."[14]

I quote Barrett at length in order to explicate the philosophical groundwork of Aiken's visions of immanence and transcendence. Neither Aiken nor Barrett influenced each other, but both began with Emersonian Transcendentalism and the work of William James and reached similar positions in middle age. The prayers found in Aiken's poetry and fiction spring from no system of thought but from a kind of instinctive cry of the soul. To achieve that instinctive cry a series of ethical decisions to continue the exploration of the soul as well as of death and chaos was necessary. Barrett is fully aware that he opens himself to the charge of mysticism, but for him this particular "mysticism" springs from a primordial psychic aspect of man: "We forget that what we call mysticism was once a natural condition of mankind, and could be again if we let ourselves enter it." Barrett thus sees the kind of creative mysticism that he advocates in terms of a modern deconstruction that has no need for logocentric systems. "The mysticism that

---

[12]William Barrett, *The Illusion of Technique* (Garden City, NY: Doubleday, 1971), 256.

[13]Ibid., 257.

[14]Ibid., 307.

matters," Barrett tells us, "is one that has no need of the word. The same with Being. Another word. We are most within Being when we do not use the word and have ceased to grapple with its idea."[15] When he is most poetic in either verse or fiction, Aiken has no need of ideas or words about Being or soul; he simply plunges his reader into the experience of soul and Being, thus sometimes projecting a sense of immanence and at other times portraying the experience of transcendence. Aiken always wanted to be a philosophical poet, and he is indeed most philosophical in the modern sense, including sometimes the deconstructive sense, when he writes about experiences of immanence and transcendence. At such moments of literary creation he more resembles Barrett or even Martin Buber or Gabriel Marcel than he does Santayana or James, both of whom maintain a kind of academic detachment not found in Aiken's best work, which is usually that work based on his existential struggle with chaos and death. Also in Aiken there is that element of heroic defiance missing in Barrett and most other modern philosophers.

Aiken saw modern problems primarily in terms of chaos and death, first in himself and then in his associates and finally in society as a whole. But the problems are not central to Aiken's vision as they usually are to Nietzsche and Heidegger, who deconstructed most of what was once Western metaphysics but who spoke in a confused manner concerning the necessary renewal of culture after the forces of chaos are pushed back enough so that life can continue. Even William Barrett lacks Aiken's heroic defiance. Barrett, caught up primarily in the modernist vision, even with his ethical and transcendental viewpoint often seems overwhelmed by various powerful modern movements: by followers of Freud who dethroned "the sovereignty of consciousness, by showing its weakness before the unconscious," by contemporary American social engineering inspired by B. F. Skinner and other behaviorists, and by the totalitarian engineering of the Russians.[16] Aiken, aware of these forces, nevertheless clung more insistently than ever to his optimistic religious beliefs as he entered an old age that became for him not a time of bitterness because of the many rejections he had received at the hands of critics and literary journalists but rather a time, as those who knew him in the sixties and seventies can all testify, of the growth of personal wisdom and a deepened literary understanding found in few writers of this century. Aiken, as I have suggested, was personally sustained in old age by the continuing study of his grandfather's sermons, but he was also

---

[15]Ibid., 318.
[16]Ibid., 316.

sustained by his visionary consciousness, which in many ways was still based at the end of his life on Romanticism. He still believed in the efficacy of both imaginative insights and in dreams as well as in the kind of Shelleyan and Yeatsian belief that through the exercise of imagination creative social existence could evolve. Like Shelley and unlike Yeats, Aiken continued to be liberal in politics until the end of his life even to campaigning for Hubert Humphrey's presidential candidacy in 1968.

As I have indicated in my article "Conrad Aiken: Resident of Savannah," Aiken was always ready to discuss his own and other people's mythic dreams. Although he was deeply aware of the world around him, Aiken occasionally reminded me, with his strong interest in vision, of William Blake. For him the pragmatic results of leading a life that affirmed both immanent and transcendent experience in himself and others was a continuing life of vision. Thus he saw himself, in no exalted manner, as one of many who were carrying on the most important historical mission of the century, that of aiding the continuing development of human consciousness. Aiken fully believed that the communal efforts of many people all over the world in this raising of human consciousness would eventually lead to a new and better era of history. He retained always Potter's optimism in the future of human beings. Aiken believed that he and Potter and others like them worked within a tradition of Romantic shamanism that has been for two centuries deepening human awareness. He believed that these individuals could, in certain visionary moments, see a new age of evolved consciousness existing in embryo in a disintegrating modern age whose decaying thought systems were still undergoing a necessary deconstruction to make way for new patterns of thought. But to approach Aiken's optimism primarily in terms of nineteenth-century Transcendentalism, as Malcolm Cowley does, is to fail to understand how the poet participates in an important modern literary tradition, that of surrealism.

Aiken himself, fully aware as he was that he had one foot in Romanticism and one in symbolism, was generally unacquainted with the surrealist movement. Except for St. John Perse and a few other modern French poets, Aiken had little use for modern French literature and, as Clarissa Lorenz reports, he never liked, at least when he was married to her, to visit Paris. Yet the leader of French surrealism, André Breton, held views on the subject of dreams and literature that were quite similar to Aiken's. As Balakian suggests, Breton, who was as strongly influenced by Freud's *The Interpretation of Dreams* as Aiken was, "foresaw as the ultimate achievement of dream study the marriage of the two states, in appearance so contradictory, of dream and reality, into one sort of absolute reality that he called surreality." Balakian goes on to say that Breton "envisaged existence as a composite of two urns, the dream and the state of wakefulness, constantly connected with each other and contributing to each other's intensity."[17]

For Balakian surrealism is a third great literary movement, one still in existence, but, like Romanticism and symbolism, one that puts vision at its center and denies the validity of logocentric thought systems. Balakian, like many other students of surrealism, believes that the real founder of the movement was not Breton but Guillaume Apollinaire, whose mission Balakian sums up:

> The power of love, the power of laughter--a very modern laughter in the face of absurdity--the mystique of fire and language, all of it fortifying the new poet with an optimism intended to erase the pessimism of the elder symbolist poets, these were to be itemized legacies that Apollinaire was to leave to his young friends, Breton, Aragon, and Soupault.[18]

Apollinaire, Breton, and Aiken all based their optimism on the shamanic belief that the modern poet's vision of paradise would eventually be realized in a new age. Thus Balakian says that Apollinaire believed that the "hymn of the future would be 'paradisiac'. . . and 'victory' had for him a more basic meaning than the cessation of hostilities."[19] The vision of paradise is basic to visionary poets from Blake and Shelley on through to the modern surrealists and expressionists.

As early as 1931 in his Expressionistic drama *The Coming Forth by Day of Osiris Jones* Aiken had announced the paradisiac theme as he showed how the anti-heroic man, Osiris Jones, would encounter chaos and, through visionary experiences, be transformed into the god-man Osiris. The play, though generally ignored (it was given a radio performance in the sixties) is a major statement in the mode of Expressionism. It contains basic themes found in Expressionism as defined, for instance, by Walter H. Sokel: "[T]he keynote of Expressionism is struck: subjectivism. Dream became

---

[17]Anna Balakian, *Surrealism: The Road to the Absolute* (New York: E. P. Dutton, 1970), 126-127.

[18]Ibid., 99.

[19]Ibid.

literature."[20] Sokel links Expressionism with surrealism through the use of dreams, pointing out that the chief inspiration of the Expressionists was Strindberg's "dream plays." For Sokel the paradisiac element is also central to Expressionism:

> With their concept of the writer as visionary and savior, the Expressionists renewed the old dream of Romanticism. Shelley's definition of the poets as "unacknowledged legislator of the world" could have been their motto.[21]

Fittingly enough, Aiken all his life believed in Shelley's concept of poet as legislator, and in doing so forecast the poet as harbinger and preparer of the new age of evolved consciousness. Yet Aiken even at the end of his life never took into account his connections with French surrealism and German Expressionism, possibly because he saw continental Europe primarily in terms of Spain and Italy. I myself tried to convince him of the many connections between *Osiris Jones* and the greatest work (I believe) of surrealist fiction in English, James Joyce's *Finnegans Wake*, which is the master's profoundest vision, written in a deconstructed dream language of humanity's entry into a new, paradisaic state. Joyce himself saw the title of Aiken's work and immediately began to seek a copy of it but never found one. In my own efforts to write about the connections between Aiken and Joyce, I talked and corresponded with the poet about *Osiris Jones*. His reply to me on this matter was thus:

> And I'm interested in your notion of doing a piece on Joyce and myself, though I wouldn't have thought of *Finnegans Wake* as being more than casually related. *Osiris Jones* I don't think he ever saw. *Time* ran a story about his three times attempting to get a copy in Paris before going off to die, but I think it never came? The resemblance to Ulysses is clearer, I think, and has now and then been overemphasized.[22]

---

[20]Walter H. Sokel, Introduction to *Anthology of German Expressionistic Drama* (Garden City, NY: Anchor Books, 1963), xxiii.

[21]Ibid.

[22]Unpublished letter, Conrad Aiken to Ted R. Spivey, September 6, 1969.

Although he never really encountered *Finnegans Wake* in its deepest sense, Aiken in *Osiris Jones*, without knowing it, had written a work basically similar to the *Wake*, one that appeared eight years before Joyce's last work was published. In it he proclaimed that through chaos humanity would receive the challenge to seek the immanent spark of God, and through an encounter with both that spark and with transcendence would renew life on earth. The play contained the old Romantic vision of poets like Blake and Shelley as well as of renegade religionists like William James Potter. Aiken as a child had first glimpsed that dream along with the dreams contained in the dark Romanticism of Poe. He cultivated both sets of dreams, and he put the two sets together in the continuing act of personal pilgrimage, which for him was the movement of the mind, the imagination (that most basic quality of the soul), and the heart (seat of the emotions) toward wider, deeper consciousness, enlightening dreams and waking visions, and (most important of all for one who suffered early a great emotional deprivation) the renewal of love, joy, hope. It is thus that I would define Aiken's concept of evolved consciousness, worked out in detail in poems, essays, novels, stories, and plays. It is essentially no different from the visions and beliefs of other significant Romantics and of some moderns, of Lawrence, Yeats, even the later Eliot. Aiken as critic approved of Eliot's *Quartets,* after rejecting his earlier religious poetry, because these works, like Aiken's Preludes, are not about belief systems but are works based on religious vision and the discovery of love.

Aiken is still remembered by those who take literature seriously, as he has been since the twenties when he first began to appear regularly in important anthologies, for works that are generally modernist in nature and specifically symbolist in viewpoint and in technique--"Tetélestai," "Silent Snow, Secret Snow," the Preludes, "Mr. Arcularis," *Ushant.* But because Aiken in twentieth-century American literature is probably second only to Pound as a figure of significant influence in the lives and works of great modernist men of letters--Eliot, Stevens, Faulkner, Lowry, Pound himself, to name only a few--it is necessary for all who would preserve the American literary tradition to take fully into account Aiken's life and work, which Aiken himself tells us many times can never be separated. Also his magnificent letters--possibly the widest ranging and most insightful of any modern American writer--must be subjected to study, and his autobiography *Ushant* still awaits assessment in relationship to other American autobiographies. Finally, Aiken still awaits discovery as a literary worker in a significant nineteenth-century stream of thought and feeling that needs large-scale reinterpretation. As I have suggested already, most of Aiken's work seems strange to contemporary critics just because it is in many ways a part of this tradition. In the sixties when parts of this tradition began to emerge in literary and student life, Aiken's stock began to go up quite suddenly, only to sink again in the seventies. But with the rediscovery of what the historian Page Smith calls the "preacherly" tradition in American education, Aiken's role as educator and philosopher will be understood. Aiken had discovered this tradition in the work of James, Santayana, Royce, and other professors at turn-of-the-century Harvard. Even to the end of his life he reminded people of an old-fashioned professor with some of the quirks of a modern writer thrown in. What the "preacherly tradition" was is thus described by Smith, himself and Southerner who went to Harvard:

> At the heart of the Protestant Passion was the conviction that individuals could know God best through the exercise of their own faculties, through 'reason' in the large and ancient meaning of the work, through mind illuminated by faith. In that effort one found aid and guidance from leaders specially trained in interpreting God's word, the elected preachers and ministers who led the elect. From John Winthrop and Roger Williams to Ralph Waldo Emerson, Horace Bushnell, Wendell Phillips, Washington Gladden, William James, Charles Sanders Pierce, and thousands of other less well-known preacher-intellectuals, religious and lay, the generality of Americans received through sermons, lectures, journals, magazines, and the public press illumination in all matters relating to manners and morals, to ethical imperatives, to social issues and public policy. With the emergence of the university as the center of intellectual activity in our society, the preacherly function of the intellectual was replaced by the priestly function. The canons of the profession held that scholarship was an essentially esoteric undertaking based on highly specialized learning and, increasingly, on an intricate 'methodology' and a technical language known only to the initiate.[23]

Smith thus makes it clear that this "preacherly" tradition began in New England but became an American phenomenon. One might add that through it Americans often learned not to look at an individual's religious or political dogmas but at the essential fact of his existence. Instead, the reasoning

---

[23]Page Smith, *Dissenting Opinions* (San Francisco: North Point Press, 1984), 121.

power, the purity of feeling, the broadness of vision of an individual came to be for many the criteria of judgment of others. For this reason Protestants, Catholics, Jews, even Buddhists, Moslems, atheists, and agnostics could find a kind of common ground in America not to be found in Europe or Asia. Aiken's lack of religious and political bigotry is one important aspect that sets him apart from friends like Eliot and Pound. He was always the American looking for the good heart and clear mind in others. And thus in *Blue Voyage* he could not only identify with but could become for a time the traveling, merchandising Jew, and in "The Poet in Granada" he could be briefly a Roman Catholic caught up in the rituals of Lorca's Spain. He could also share the experiences of others and at the same time still be a rebel against all systems of thought and belief. The heart, not the belief, was for him the important matter in life. Often identifying with that shadowy early Bostonian William Blackstone, Aiken was thus a quintessential American, one might even say an American original, like and unlike all the Americans who sought in the new nation a goodness denied them in older lands.

The American thinker of his own period that Aiken resembles in many ways is the best known American theologian of the century, Reinhold Niebuhr, himself a second generation German-American, and a representative of what Smith calls the preacherly tradition in higher education. Niebuhr and Aiken both were significant members of the American liberal tradition who in part were followers of William James. Yet both discovered for themselves the complexities of the human heart and soul, and both accepted the element of chaos that always exists within the individual and his community. Both, because of their own deeply felt experiences, were inevitably driven to accept a view of God that was both transcendent and immanent. Aiken thus in his attitude toward God reminds us of what Niebuhr's biographer Richard Fox says of the theologian: "The God Niebuhr knew he needed was at once transcendent and immanent. Transcendent enough to leave human beings their individuality and to enter a 'relationship' with them. Immanent enough to empower then to act freely and responsibly, the only kind of action that benefit 'persons.'"[24] For Niebuhr religious certainty "had to be grounded in a philosophy of human needs and in the actual experience of belief."[25] No better descriptions of Aiken's own

---

[24]Richard Wightman Fox, *Reinhold Niebuhr: A Biography* (New York: Pantheon Books, 1985), 117.

[25]Ibid.

sense of the immanence and transcendence and of his personal religious belief of God could be given.

Like Niebuhr, Aiken believed that for religion to be effective it had to be closely connected with the mystery of personality. "Niebuhr's preoccupation with 'personality' was typical of liberal Protestant thinkers in both America and Germany," Fox writes.[26] Aiken too as a personalist, a follower of Whitman and Emerson, exalted the centrality of the total individual in all his work. Yet, unlike Niebuhr, Aiken retained to the end of his life a profound vision of the continuing evolution of human consciousness that Niebuhr lacked. Aiken, even more than Niebuhr, had broken through the suffering of an early life and had discovered a vision on the other side of mental distress. That vision gave Aiken an optimism few modern poets and thinkers have known. It is a vision that still awaits a wide acceptance.

---

[26]Ibid., 21.

Epilogue:

The Quest for Home

The most important single fact of Conrad Aiken's life was the loss of his home and family at the age of eleven. He himself made this clear whenever he discussed his life and work, which he often did, always linking the life with the work. Literature was the chief means he chose to combat the psychic pain that sprang from early loss, but for him the best of his writing-- and he often was not at his best--grew always from the deepest aspects of what he would eventually call his "divine pilgrimage." He was always the quester, the traveler on a spiritual journey, and this face, together with the shamanic aspects of his work that spring in large part from the influence of Wordsworth and Shelley, gave his major work many characteristics of a Romanticism that was basic to his literary existence. Yet as one who fully accepted modernism, Aiken also plunged into the forest of symbols existing both in his psyche and in his own and other's work. He rightly saw the symbolist movement as the advance guard of modernism's efforts to come to terms not only with chaos and death but also with symbol, myth, and a necessary renewal of language. Aiken felt also the tug of the deconstructing forces that were strong throughout that modernistic period, in which, in spite of searches for a postmodernism, we are still living. As a modernist Aiken deconstructed both forms and contents, but as a Romantic he preserved much from the past, and at the same time he sought to recompose literary, psychological, and philosophical viewpoints. Through a return to his inherited Unitarianism, always a philosophically and theologically deconstructing religious persuasion that he had partially let go, Aiken managed in his last years to settle upon a viewpoint that mediated between a Romantic past and a modern present. Yet up to the time of his death--and beyond--Aiken presented himself to the world as a quester.

Malcolm Cowley has suggested that Aiken finally settled into a kind of Emersonian Transcendentalism, and he cites what he believes to be Aiken's last poem, "Obituary in Bitcherel," to prove that Aiken was really a New England poet. For Cowley Aiken was a "reckless and fanciful New England voice" (--*And I Worked at the Writer's Trade*, 231). Yet few if any critics today would place Aiken alongside New England poets like Robert Frost or Edwin Arlington Robinson. If anything, as primarily a follower, as a man of letters, of Edgar Allan Poe and as a close friend of Allen Tate's, Aiken was a transatlantic poet who often mediated as critic, fiction writer, and poet between Europe and America. He also mediated between the North and the South, and yet he could well be called a writer of the Atlantic seaboard. He knew the many connections between cities like Boston and Savannah, and he records in *Ushant* his remembrances of going by sea back and forth between these two cities. In my own conversations with Aiken I found he knew little of the Georgia beyond Savannah, but for that matter he knew very little about the great American spaces beyond the Atlantic seacoast, though in some lesser works he tried, Whitman-like, to capture a sense of the wholeness of America. Yet at his best Aiken wrote about certain cities and certain houses, particularly the one house in Savannah where his pilgrimage began.

In England, Clarissa Lorenz tells us, Aiken was generally thought of as a Southern poet. When in the early 1960s Dean Kenneth M. England of Georgia State University wrote Aiken to ask if he were indeed a Southern poet, he received the cryptic reply that the poet planned to be buried in Savannah's Bonaventure Cemetery. Yet if one knows of Aiken's quest for an ever deeper possession of a few places, then he might not be surprised at this answer. Three houses were continually sought in Aiken's imagination and in his literary works--Jeake's House in Rye, Forty-One Doors in Brewster, and above all, the Regency House in Savannah. But there was always in Aiken's mind and work the fourth house in Bonaventure Cemetery, where his father and mother resided together. Aiken lacked Poe's morbidity about the grave and death. A writer of limericks like Aiken could never be a death's-head Romantic. Nevertheless, Aiken when in Savannah would pour a libation of wine on his parent's tombstone in remembrance of their birth. And for his own grave, located next to theirs, he provided a marble bench so that visitors might have a picnic as he had sometimes had at his parents' gravesite. The two epitaphs on the bench sum up much that was basic to the life of Conrad Aiken.

One epitaph speaks of the poet's quest continuing after death: "Cosmos Mariner/ Destination Unknown." The other tells of what for Aiken was the great virtue, that form of love he called *caritas*. It says simply: "Give my love to the world." In 1979 Mary Hoover Aiken told me that her husband spoke these words once when he thought he was dying, but did not. She told him that she would put the words on his tombstone. The other epitaph came from the name of a ship that the Aikens on their daily walk from Oglethorpe Street to the Savannah River saw passing out to sea. Looking up the name of the ship in the newspaper to see what port it was bound for, they read

"Destination Unknown." Thus the epigraphs sum up a large part of Aiken's mature wisdom. For Aiken the divine pilgrimage meant the giving and receiving of love, two acts which for him summed up the essence of authentic religious experience. The pilgrimage itself was cosmic in nature, continuing beyond one life, and the ultimate destination could never be known, though that destination was for Aiken the individual's ultimate home, a destination reflected in the temporary homes of everyone's life's journey.

That Aiken did have a sense of a divine pilgrimage continuing after his death can be seen in what Joseph Killorin believed was in fact the last poem he wrote, an unrevised work written, as Killorin puts it, "on Oglethorpe Avenue in Savannah four months before his death" (*Selected Letters of Conrad Aiken*, 206). The poem begins with a statement concerning the poet's triumph over death: "Death is a toy upon the nursery floor/ broken we know that it can hurt no more." Then he speaks of spiritual rebirth, which "begins to seem/ like that recurring and delicious dream/ of middle age." The dream is about Atlantis, a land "where we paused to rest/ and saw the sacred people of the west," who are "Angelic beings through and through." Aiken had written in earlier poems of a sacred realm he could briefly experience from time to time in dream and vision. In no other poem does he record so intense an experience of that sacred realm which shamans traditionally have glimpsed in their visions of divine glory. The result of this experience for the poet is his memory that "we heard the mystics, saw the mysteries so that now we turn once more/ to look at death upon the nursery floor" (*Selected Letters*, 206). In no other poem by Aiken is there so positive a statement about the overcoming of death. At the end of a long life Aiken looks back in this poem to see that his pilgrimage had indeed overcome death, revealing it to be a toy lying upon a child's nursery floor. And, the poem seems to say, human existence in our time is but the nursery period of a long journey leading to that full development of consciousness that Aiken believed to be humanity's ultimate destiny.

To the end Aiken believed he had faithfully played a role in the development of consciousness, and his last letter, dictated as Killorin tells us to Mary Aiken on July 30, 1973, answers a Michigan high school student who wrote him praising "The Morning Song of Lord Zero," saying that "none of us knows in what direction poetry and the other arts will turn--that's part of the cruel fascination of being interested in the arts as you are, and keeping your head about it." He then adds, "If there is anything good in my poetry people like yourself will find it" (*Selected Letters*, 331). Aiken died on the afternoon of August 17, 1973 in the Oglethorpe Avenue house located next door to the house he lived in as a child. He was twelve days into his eighty-fourth year.

Aiken visited Savannah in 1936 for the first time since he had left as a child of eleven. In 1901, before his father began to lose his mind, with death heavy in a heart set on being a poet in the "liberal" tradition of an earlier Romanticism, Aiken never gave up his early Romanticism. But he did take fully upon himself the inherited task of modernism to face fully humankind's irrational side and to take into account chaos and death in their personal and social aspects. The poet's last letter records, as did so much of his later life, a Romantic optimism he had known as a young child and a calm acceptance of anything the future might hold. Through much suffering he had found his way home to that faith in humanity's continuing evolution that he had inherited from his Unitarian and Quaker forefathers.

Many people with whom Aiken had conversed in the years after World War II remember the faith and wisdom the poet had achieved. In 1967 I was talking with Aiken in a room whose wall separated us from the house next door, where his childhood had been blown apart sixty-six years before. I said something about his long pilgrimage, and Aiken answered, as he pointed to the wall: "It began right over there." I asked him about the pain of it all and, without answering, he smiled a rich, hieratic smile of an ancient man of wisdom, a smile that said that death indeed had been overcome.